W9-BHR-752

HOVSTON
PVBLIC LIBRARY

Gift of

Edna Joseph Fund

AN INTRODUCTION TO THE SKILL OF MUSICK

Da Capo Press Music Reprint Series
GENERAL EDITOR: FREDERICK FREEDMAN
Vassar College

AN INTRODUCTION TO THE SKILL OF MUSICK

By John Playford

The Twelfth Edition

Corrected and Amended by
Henry Purcell

With Selected Chapters from the Thirteenth and Fourteenth Editions

New Introduction, Glossary, and Index by
Franklin B. Zimmerman, *University of Pennsylvania*

DA CAPO PRESS • NEW YORK • 1972

R01 0339 9814

Library of Congress Cataloging in Publication Data

Playford, John, 1623-1686 ?
An introduction to the skill of musick.

(Da Capo Press music reprint series)
Reprint of the 12th ed., 1694, "corrected and amended by Henry Purcell. With selected chapters from the thirteenth and fourteenth editions."
Includes bibliographical references.
1. Music—Manuals, text-books, etc.—To 1800.
2. Violin—Instruction and study. 3. Viola da gamba.
4. Counterpoint. I. Purcell, Henry, 1658 or 9-1695.
II. Title.
MT7.P75 1972 780 67-27551
ISBN 0-306-70937-6

This Da Capo Press reprint of *An Introduction to the Skill of Musick* is an unabridged republication of the Twelfth Edition published in London in 1694. It includes in addition supplementary material taken from the other twenty-two versions of the work, as well as a new introduction, a glossary of musical terms, and an index prepared by Franklin B. Zimmerman. To facilitate reference to the index, new pagination has been assigned throughout. In the original text sections, this new pagination is set in brackets outside the original pagination.

© 1972 by Da Capo Press, Inc.
A Subsidiary of Plenum Publishing Corporation
227 West 17th Street, New York, New York 10011

All Rights Reserved

Manufactured in the United States of America

73P 08270

Contents

Introduction

John Playford (b. Norwich, 1623; d. London, *c.* Nov., 1686)[1] appeared on the musical scene in London in March of 1640 as an apprentice to John Benson, music publisher and bookseller, who had recently moved from Chancery Lane to St. Dunstan's Church Yard in Fleet Street.[2] In April of 1647, Playford finished his apprenticeship, and he soon obtained a master-printer's ticket from the Stationer's Company. Shortly thereafter, aged about twenty-five, he set up his own publishing and bookselling shop "in the Inner Temple, neere the Church doore" just opposite St. Dunstan's.

Here he began in the music-publishing trade, in cooperation rather than in competition with his former printing-master, Benson. Five of his earliest music publications appeared under their joint imprint.[3] Meanwhile, in collaboration with Peter Cole and Francis Tyton in Cornhill, Playford also had printed various Royalist political pamphlets, whose immediate result was a warrant for the arrest of all three men. With the restoration of the Stuart monarchy in

---

1. According to Harry M. Wilsher, *Grove's Dictionary of Music and Musicians,* 5th edition (London, Macmillan, 1954), Vol. VI, p. 825.

2. The indenture, dated March 23rd, is cited by Margaret Dean-Smith in her introduction to the facsimile edition of Playford's *The English Dancing Master* (London, Schott & Co., 1957), p. xii. (See fn. 3, below, for the full text of the original title page.)

3. *A Musicall Banquet* (London, Printed by T. H[arper] for John Benson and John Playford, 1651); *Musica Harmonia* (*ibid.,* 1651); *Musick and Mirth* (*ibid.,* 1651; these first three books appeared as parts I, II, and III within a single binding, 1651); *Catch that Catch Can* (London, Benson and Playford, 1652; but printed in the previous year, according to Frank Kidson, "John Playford and 17th Century Music Publishing," *The Musical Quarterly,* Vol. IV, No. 2 [April, 1918], p. 522); *A Booke of New Lessons for the Cithern and Gittern* (London, Benson and Playford, 1652); and *A Booke of New Lessons for the Gittern* (London, Benson and Playford, 1652). However, Playford seems to have published by himself his famous book of English dances which appeared that same year, as the title page indicates: *The English Dancing Master:/OR,/*Plaine and easie Rules for the Dancing of Country Dances, with the Tune to each Dance./[Vignette]/ *LONDON,/*Printed by *Thomas Harper,* and are to be sold by *John Playford,* at his Shop in the Inner/Temple neere the Church doore. 1651. (Facsimile edition, London, Schott & Co., 1957). Except for a few publications upon which he collaborated with Zachariah Watkins in 1664 and 1665, Playford was sole publisher for all the remainder of his impressive production.

1660, however, such warrants lost their effectiveness. Moreover, Tory pamphleteering was no longer politically culpable, but rather the opposite, as may be seen from the open manner in which the three men summarized their protests, publishing in the first year of the Restoration the renowned pamphlet, *England's Black Tribunal.*

From about 1652 onward, "Honest John" Playford—as he soon was known[4]—established himself as the most important seller and publisher of music in England. For thirty-four years during the Commonwealth and Restoration periods he was responsible for a large share of the entire English production of printed music. Though he was by no means the first important music publisher in London, Playford's title as "the Father of English music publishing" has some justification.[5] The quality, as well as the quantity of his publications, and especially his integrity as an editor, established for him a reputation equaled by very few in England.

Besides numerous other successful songbooks and songbook series,[6] and several instrumental collections,[7] Playford edited such highly popular method books as *The English Dancing Master,* which ran to eighteen editions between 1651 and 1728; *Apollo's Banquet,* which began about 1669 a series of pieces for violin, utilizing works printed in the third edition of the *Dancing Master;*[8] and *Musick's Recreation on the Lyra Viol,* four editions of which appeared between 1652 and 1682. In 1654 he published the first edition of his most influential English method book, indeed the most influential of the century: *A Breefe Introduction to the Skill of Musick for Song and Violl.*

An expansion of musical rules printed earlier in *A Musicall Banquet,* the *Introduction* was reedited for seventeen or eighteen issues—depending on whether or not one counts the missing or,

4. Kidson, *op. cit.,* p. 516. See also, Lillian M. Ruff, "A Survey of John Playford's 'Introduction to the Skill of Music,'" *The Consort,* No. 22, Summer, 1965, p. 37.

5. Margaret Dean-Smith identifies Frank Kidson as the author of this epithet, and comments on its aptness in her Introduction to the facsimile reprint of Playford's *The English Dancing Master,* pp. x and xii.

6. Such as *Select Musicall Ayres and Dialogues* (by Wilson, Coleman, William Lawes, and others, 1652); Henry Lawes's *Ayres and Dialogues* (1653); Hilton's *Catch that Catch Can* (1652); William Child's *Choice Musick to the Psalms of David* (1656); *etc.*

7. *A Musicall Banquet* (1651); *A Booke of New Lessons for the Cithern and Gittern* (1652); *Musick's Recreation on the Lyra Viol* (1652); *etc.*

8. Kidson, *op. cit.,* p. 520.

more likely, nonexistent ninth edition—and saw altogether twenty-two reprintings in the seventy-six years between 1654 and 1730. It served four generations of English musicians as a handbook and, in the course of its life, spanned two of the lowest points in the history of native English music, and one of the most flourishing as well.

The ninth of Playford's musical publications, chronologically speaking, the *Introduction to the Skill of Musick* provided not merely a single method, but rather a compendium of methods, more or less as had its prototype, *A Musicall Banquet.* The component parts of the *Introduction* varied in number throughout its many printings, each being subject at all times to deletion, emendation, revision, or substitution, or to several of these processes in combination. Thus, throughout the Commonwealth and Restoration periods this ever-changing handbook was available to each generation of English musicians in several different versions, each reflecting the latest in foreign and domestic musical fashions without departing essentially from England's conservative musical traditions. The innovations, the experiments, and the new influences from abroad which helped to produce the impressive expansion of English musical life after 1660 were all reflected in the pages of the successive editions;[9] and each new issue helped both to confirm and to spread the conventions and changes represented in its pages to another generation of English musicians.

The first *Introduction* of 1654, consisting of Playford's foreword, eight chapters, and several appendices, among them Thomas Campion's "A Preface, or a Brief Discourse of the nature and use of the Scale or Gam-ut," actually grew out of an earlier publication, as Playford indicated in the note to the reader included in his *Court-Ayres: OR/Pavins, Almains, Corant's, and Sarabands*...of 1655:

> *To all Understanders and LOVERS of MUSICK./*
> About three years since I published a Booke called the *Musicall Banquet,* there/being in it a small taste of

9. The chronological distribution and groupings of these make an interesting index of England's musical activity throughout the years in question, which may be divided, roughly, into four generations: In the first (1654–1667), nine versions of the *Introduction* appeared; in the second (1670–1687), there were six; in the third (1694–1713), five; and in the fourth (1718–1730), only three. These statistics mirror the musical needs of the nation, and, in addition, the rise and decline of native creative vigor throughout the crucial period in the history of English music extending from Cromwellian times well into the Handelian period.

> Musick in four severall Tracts. The first was some/ *Rules for Song and Violl.* The second had in it about 30 Lessons for *Lyra Violl.*/The third contained about 27 lessons of *Two Parts, Basse* and *Treble.* And/the fourth consisted of about 20 *Rounds* and *Catches.*// That little Booke finding such acceptance among all Lovers and Practitio-/ners in Musick (and the Impression now totally sold off) I resolved to inlarge/each of these Tracts, and to Print them in severall Books, which I have now/(through Gods permission) accomplish'd. The first Book I call, *A brief Intro-/duction to the skill of Song and Violl.* The second, *Musicks Recreation,* wherein is 117 Lessons for the/*Lyra Violl.* The third is intituled *Court-Ayres of two parts Treble and Basse,* containing 246 Lessons./The fourth is called *Catch that Catch Can, or Catches, Rounds, and Cannons,* for 3 or foure Voyces,/containing at least 150. Whereby you have a much larger Banquet than you had before.//...

From such scant beginning was to develop the musical handbook "more generally purchased and read, than any elementary musical tract that ever appeared in this or any other country."[10] The long-lost first edition of 1654 was slimmer by half than any of the eighteen or so to follow. Yet, compared to the original treatise, it seems a fairly ambitious publication. Its eight chapters and several appendices (occupying less than forty pages in all) established the format for later editions, although Playford continued to make changes in every new issue. The title page and preface, and a table of contents (here made up for the first time) will suffice to show the scope of Playford's essay:

> A/Breefe/INTRODUCTION/to the Skill/of/MUSICK/for/Song & Violl/by JP/London Printed/1654/ Sould by/Jo: Playford/at his shop/in the Inner/ Temple//[11]

10. Charles Burney, *A General History of Music,* ed. F. Mercer (New York, Dover, 1957), Vol. II, p. 330.

11. As pointed out by the anonymous author of *Playford's Brief Introduction to the Skill of Musick: An Account with Bibliographical Notes of An Unique Collection comprising all the editions from 1654 to 1730 in the possession of Messrs. Ellis* (London, 1926), the handsome border was that used by Slatyer for his publication of Psalms in 1643.

[Sig. A2] To all Lovers & Practitioners/OF/MUSICK./Courteous Reader:/I was desired by some Masters to/Print the Scale of Musick,/or Gam-ut, in a halfe sheet of/Paper, to put in a Schollers Book, to save the pains of wri-/ting; which I intended onely/to have done; but upon second thoughts I have/altred my minde, and made the addition of some/necessary plain Rules for the better understand-/ing thereof, and the help of Beginners. I confess,/men better able then my selfe might have spared/my pains, but their slownesse and modesty (being/as I conceive unwilling to appear in Print about/so small a matter) hath put me upon the Worke,/which I count very usefull, though with the dan-/ger of not being so well done, as they might have/ performed it.[12] The Rules of all Arts ought to bee/ delivered in plaine and briefe language, and not/with flowers of Eloquence; and so this Worke is/more sutable to my abilities./The Work as it is I must confesse is not all my/owne, some part of it was collected out of other/mens writings, which I hope will the more com-/mend it: and if the brevity, plainnesse, and usefulnesse thereof may beget acceptance with/thee, it will encourage me to do thee more service/in other things of this nature./

Thine to the utmost
of his endeavours,
John Playford.

12. Playford seems to have forgotten about this explanation when he wrote the Preface to his *Court-Ayres* (as quoted above) in the following year. However, the two explanations are not necessarily mutually exclusive.

The success of this first slender but comprehensive method for general musical instruction may be gauged by the small amount of time which elapsed before the second edition appeared—just a year.[14] For England, whose musical foundations had been undermined systematically for nearly twenty years, the need to reestablish a general pedagogical basis for the fundamentals of music was urgent. The demands created by this widespread need may be measured, so far as concerns their effect, by the short time in which the first edition was exhausted, and by the manner in which some two dozen new issues followed in rapid succession during the succeeding decades. These, and the changes they underwent, in turn reveal the importance of the part assumed by Playford's *Introduction* in the restora-

---

12a. Borrowed "out of Mr. Butler's learned Treatise," as Playford honestly admits. As Lillian Ruff has pointed out *op. cit.*, p. 37), Playford borrowed also from William Barley's anonymous publication, *The Pathway to Musicke* and from Morley's *Plain and Easy Introduction.*

13. This table of contents does not appear in Playford's edition. The two-part "Almaine" mentioned in the next to last line probably was written by Alfonso Ferrabosco II, who had been dead for a quarter of a century. However, it is just possible that the piece may have been composed by Alfonso III, still active at court at the time this work was published as violinist and wind-instrument player (cf. *Grove's Dictionary* (5th edition), Vol. III, pp. 67–69).

14. Playford's statement in his preface to the *Court-Ayres* makes it quite clear that the first edition sold out completely and quickly. (See pp. 9-10 above.)

tion of English music; and, in fact, it was directly involved in the processes which led to the flourishing musical life, which Henry Purcell knew and enhanced so well.

The 1655 printing, for a time considered the first edition, included a revised version of most of Thomas Campion's important treatise, *A New Way of Making Fowre parts in Counterpoint, by a most familiar and infallible rule.* Campion had mooted a theory of triadic inversion as early as 1613, more than a century before Rameau formulated the same principle in his *Traité de l'harmonie* (1722),[15] and his treatise, now emended and brought up to date by Christopher Simpson, added very significantly to the usefulness and importance of Playford's *Introduction.*

Unaccountably omitted in 1658, Campion's revised treatise reappeared in the edition of 1660, this time under the title, *The Art of Setting or Composing Music in Parts.* Curiously, the title pages of 1660 and 1664 also offered a simplified alternative title for the treatise—*The Art of Descant*—while the 1662 edition retained the principal title alone on a separate title page (dated 1661). The simplified title became dominant, however, and continued to be used in all editions and reprints until 1683, when the whole of the third part was anonymously rewritten with heavy reliance upon Christopher Simpson's *A Compendium of Practical Music,* printed in London by Henry Brome just five years earlier. This section[16] was reprinted without alteration in the eleventh edition of 1687, otherwise known mainly for its long elegy to Playford, whose death had so saddened the English musical community in November of the preceding year. In the twelfth edition of 1694, "corrected and amended by Henry Purcell" (as the announcement on the main title page shows), the third book (*The Art of Descant, etc.*) reached its best-known form.[17]

15. Manfred Bukofzer's evaluation of Campion's formulation (in his Preface to Coperario's *Rules How to Compose* [Los Angeles, Gottlieb, 1951]) was perhaps overenthusiastic, as Henry Gibbons has pointed out in *Observations on A New Way of Making Fowre Parts in Counter-point by Thomas Campion* (Unpublished Master's Thesis, Harvard, 1964), p. 29.

16. From the so-called tenth edition of 1683—"so-called" because a ninth edition has never been found, and may not have existed.

17. It is possible that Purcell may have made some corrections and emendations for the thirteenth edition (1697) before his death in November of 1695. But someone else must have rewritten and revised the treatise as a whole. (However, the third book was left almost exactly as Purcell wrote it.)

Meanwhile other portions of the original treatise had also undergone changes and revisions from edition to edition. In the second edition (1655), Playford had appended to the eight original chapters a ninth on musical notation and a tenth on "Tuning the voice," at the same time enlarging the "Introduction to plaine and easie directions for the Violl de Gambo" and adding a new, much longer preface. Playford devoted the last few pages of this edition to "Questions propounded by the Doctors in/Musick, to have been discussed in the/Act at Oxford, *July 8* 1622./Mr. *Nathanial Gyles,* Resp./ Mr. William Heather Opp."/The questions are perhaps interesting enough for an academic occasion; but except for those applying to the third of the following items, none of the discussions seems interesting enough today to merit quotation here:

1. *Whether Discords may be allowed in Musick?/* Aff[irmative]./
2. *Whether any artificial Instrument can so fully/and truly express Musick as the naturall/voyce?* Neg[ative]./
3. *Whether the Practick be the more usefull part/of Musick, or the Theory?* Aff[irmative]/ . . .

The Objection to the third Question./

The true difference between an Art and a Science/ is that an Art is more subject to sence, and requires/the use of some outward Demonstration, and a Sci-/ence is properly the subject of the intellectual fa-/culty, But Musick is rather one of the seven liberal/Sciences then an Art, *Ergo,* the Theory of Musick is/the more usefull part of Musick then the Practick./

Answ. I deny the minor, Musick is both an Art,/and a Science; as it is a Science, so it maketh use of/Arithmeticall, Geometricall, and Musicall propor-/tion according to the five kindes, that is to say,/*Multiplex, Super particularie, Super partiens;/Multiplex Super particulary,* and *Multiplex Super par-/tiens,* But as it is an Art which requireth artifi-/ciall Demonstration, so it is usefull, for the many/ends thereof, either for modest mirth and recrea-/tion, as Pavins, Galliards, Almains, Coranto's, Le-/volta's, Mottets, Madrigals,

> Ayres, Jigges, &c./Wherein use is made of those musicall Moods, cal-/led *Dorian, Phrygian, Mixolidian, Ionick,* and/the rest of those kindes, or more especially for set-/ting forth the glory of God in Psalmes, Hymns,/ and spirituall/Songs, the Antiquity whereof, the/holy Scriptures of God, both in the Old and New/Testament do famously record, and so great hath/been and is, the Practicall use thereof in Gods/Church and House of Prayer, as also in other holy/Assemblies, that such reverence and estimation in/places, and at all times hath been given, to the Ma-/sters and Professors thereof (especially in this King-/dome of *England*) as that the most noble Universi-/ties have dignifi'd no one of the liberall Sciences/with the Degree and Title of Doctorship, but only/Musick./FINIS.//

In the unnumbered edition of 1658 Playford again revised the Preface, enlarged Chapter IV, added two new chapters, and appended the section, "Short Hymns and Psalms fit for the practice of Young Learners." Campion's *Art of Setting*... was omitted, possibly to make room for this new material.

As if to celebrate the Restoration, the "third Edition, Enlarged" of 1660 was graced by R. Gaywood's engraved portrait of Playford at the age of 38. The engraving also shows two winged figures holding an open music book displaying a setting of the celebratory Psalm, *Cantate Domino.* In Playford's hand is a page on which is written the beginning of a famous canonic melody, "Non nobis Domine."

This edition included Campion's treatise (with additions by Simpson), which is called a "third book," possibly to justify Playford's opinion that it was the legitimate successor to those of Thomas Morley and Charles Butler, which had long since gone out of print. Playford also added two-part "Ayres or Songs" by Thomas Brewer Campion, Dowland, the Lawes brothers, Jeremy Savile, William Webbe, and John Wilson; Byrd's canon, "Non nobis" (here anonymous), which had figured in the frontispiece; and another *à 6,* "Joy in the Gates of Jerusalem."[17a] In addition, this abundant edition included Charles Colman's "Table of graces proper to the Violl or Violin."

The reprint of 1662 (with a portrait engraving by D. Loggan) was followed by the thoroughly revised and "much enlarged" fourth edition of 1664, with Gaywood's engraved portrait of Playford,

17a. Miss Ruff has traced this composition to Thomas Ravenscroft's *Pammelia,* 1609. *Op. cit.,* p. 40.

"Ætatis Suae 40 An° Domino 1663," over the following quatrain:

> This, Playford's Shadow doth present,
> Peruse his Booke and there you'll see
> His whole Designe is Publique Good
> His Soule and Minde an Harmonie.

(The close similarity of this portrait to that of 1660 suggests that it was not engraved anew from life and that, consequently, Playford's age, as given in the inscription, cannot be taken at face value.)

This edition is especially significant for introducing the historically important, though by then somewhat dated,

> A Brief Discourse of, and Directions/for Singing after the Italian manner:/Wherein is set down those Excellent/Graces in Singing now used by the/Italians: Written some time since by/an English Gentleman who lived many/years in Italy, and Taught the same/here in England; intending to publish the/same, but prevented by Death.//

Playford's "anonymous Gentleman" had borrowed most of this straight from Giulio Caccini's epoch-making *Le Nuove Musiche,* published in Florence in 1601. As has been observed frequently, Italian influence was indeed important for the reconstruction of English music after the Commonwealth; but that it was of older vintage than has generally been supposed is again verified here.[18]

Although the Preface was shortened, and the discussion of Greek modes omitted, the "Brief Discourse" filled all the space thus saved and more. Further expansion resulted from the addition of a general essay on music and its "Divine and Civil uses."

There is little essential difference between this "fourth enlarged" edition of 1664 and the unnumbered edition which appeared that same year (probably later). Most of the apparent disparities were due, it would seem, to careless typesetting and poor proofreading in the numbered edition. The resulting lapses were corrected in the unnumbered edition—hence this writer's guess that it is the later—but mistakes in pagination occur even there. Apparently, members of Playford's working crew were not always up to the fine standards he had established, pp. 69-78 being hopelessly confused.

18. See below, pp. 25-7. Here Playford included a setting in Caccini's "Recitative style" of the English text "Oh, that mine eyes would melt into a Floud," to demonstrate that this manner of singing might be "used to our English words as well as Italian." For a reproduction of the song, see Ian Spink, "Playford's 'Directions for Singing after the Italian Manner," *Monthly Musical Record,* Vol. 89, No. 994, July-August, 1959, p. 132.

After the next two issues (1666, 1667), the unnumbered fifth edition, now shortened by omission of several of the airs, appeared in 1670. In the Houghton Library copy, a contemporary hand has added over the "York Tune" for *Psalm* 73 (p. 54) the interesting MS note, "Said to be composed by the Great Milton." This edition is graced by two new engravings. One (by F. H. van Hove) shows Playford, now forty-seven and appearing somewhat older, while the other, signed "W. S.," depicting a bass-viol performer in action, replaces the engraving of the instrument alone printed previously.

The sixth edition of 1672 returned to the earlier engraving of the bass-viol but retained van Hove's portrait.[19] To the material in the 1670 edition, this added "A table of the Comparison of the Cliffs," restored the chapter on Greek modes, and revived at least ten of the "short ayres," which, unaccountably, had dwindled to two in the three prior impressions. William Lawes's "Gather ye rosebuds" and J. G[amble's] "Will Cloris cast her sunbright eye," which had endured, were now joined by such songs as Thomas Morley's "Now is the month of Maying," and Playford's own "Come, Swain, why sitt'st thou." Like van Hove's portrait engraving, only slightly retouched and labeled "ætat 57" for its final impression in the tenth edition of 1683, these tunes were reprinted throughout the intervening decade, brightening with their simple charm the gray theoretical matter around them.

The seventh edition of 1674, again "corrected and enlarged," gave a revised set of "Rules and Directions for Singing Psalms" and added "The Order of Performing the Divine Service in Cathedrals and Collegiate Chappels," taken from (but not acknowledged to) Edward Lowe's recent publication on the same subject.[20] A "carefully corrected" eighth edition[21] of 1679 shows few changes. The

19. In the Houghton Library copy an inscription under the portrait—apparently in a contemporary hand—reads: "Born 1613, died 1693, aged 80 years." Interesting, if unaccountable, in view of past confusion as to the date of Playford's death. Interestingly, the portrait, while similar in general configuration, had been reengraved, mainly, it would seem, to render pleasant the very dour, worried expression on Playford's face in the original.

20. *A Short Direction for the Performance of Cathedrall Service* (Oxford: 1661), followed by "A Review" of the same which he published in (Oxford: 1664).

21. The only corrections which leap to the eye appear to be the removal of the rather embarrassing typographical blunder on the previous main title page—"Instruments [for "Instructions"] for the Treble Violin"—

ninth (1681?), which is not extant, may never have been printed. For the tenth edition of 1683, it seems, from the quotation to follow, that Playford himself completely rewrote Campion's "Art of Descant," describing the new version as "a more Plain and Easie Method than any heretofore Published." At the end he reemphasized his singleness of purpose in seeking practical simplicity and clarity as follows:

> To conclude this Part of the Art of Composing/Musick: My endeavour has been to set forth only/what is most useful for the Practitioner, rather/by necessary Examples than long Discourses and/Precepts: In the whole, you will meet many/Examples not to be found in other Books; I must/confess, (being streightned for Time) I could/not so Methodically put it into that order I inten-/ded: However, if what I have here done meet/with a kind reception, it will encourage me, (if/ God permit Life for another Impression) to amend/ what faults are committed in this. *Vale*/ J. P.//[21a]

Faults to amend seem few indeed, and the treatise as a whole strikes one as well-conceived and carefully executed. Besides Byrd's "Non nobis Domine," mentioned above, there are several new pieces in the text proper, including two four-part examples of "canon in the unison on a plain Song," and an interesting three-part canon, "Ut queant laxis." These increase the value of this version greatly, as does Playford's careful elaboration of the mechanics of counterpoint. But its chief merit lies in the above-mentioned refreshing simplicity and clarity, achievements which Playford's younger contemporary, Henry Purcell, was doing so much to parallel just at that time in the stylistic renovation of English music.

Playford's premonition, as expressed in the passage cited above, was all too sound, for he died in November of 1686. His eleventh edition appeared the next year, but this does not mean that he had died before preparations for its publication were begun or perhaps

---

and the sorting out of various rubrics which somehow got muddled in the new "Order of Performing the Divine Service. . . ." Besides these, there are a few inconsequential emendations and some tightening up of the prose style. Playford's remarks on the essay on Italian singing were omitted, and unaccountably, Campion's treatise, recently elevated to the status of "Book Three," appears here again simply as The ART of/DESCANT:/ OR,/*Composing of Musick in Parts.*/

21a. Lillian Ruff provides a complete list of Playford's borrowings, identifying sources. *Op. cit.*, p. 43.

even well underway. Whether or not he had found time to amend the faults he had found in the tenth edition is a moot point. At any rate, there is no evidence to indicate what he may have had in mind, for there are no corrections or emendations of any kind. In fact, the only differences are to be found in the insertion of a new canon, *Gloria Patri,* "Three Parts in One" (pp. 42–44), of Purcell's canon, "Four in Two," on *Miserere* (p. 45: z 109), in the deletion of Playford's note of apology at the end of the tenth edition, and in a revision of the list of "Musick Books Sold by John Playford," now inventoried under Henry's name and printed with a page devoted to "Other Books sold at the same Shop."

Considering future developments, one of the most significant passages in the eleventh edition has to do with an Italian compositional technique which Playford made special point of including, despite his earlier expression of xenophobic sentiments on musical borrowing:

> Also if you take two *Sevenths* so the one be *minor,* and the other *Major,* it is allowed, but be sure the *Minor* be set before the *Major,* as you see in the Example.

7
7
7
7

> I have often observed in several late *Italian Au-/thors,* where Figures are placed over the *Thorough-/Bass,* that 6 or 7 *Sevenths* have followed each other,/which has been much wondred at by some Young/Composers, and for their satisfaction I have inserted/this example, which shows both the method and/manner how it is performed.//

Conjecture as to who these young composers may have been would be idle. Henry Purcell was too well established, even in 1683, to be referred to in this manner. Yet, as shall be shown later, this kind of interest in Italian style and technique was clearly evident in the two editions of Playford's "Third Book" with which Purcell was involved. Certainly, his twelfth edition (to be discussed separately in greater detail below) shows specific interest on Purcell's part in Playford's little Italianate paradigm, if only a negative interest, because the passage and example are both deleted.

For the thirteenth edition of 1697, Henry Playford commissioned someone to revise and reorganize the whole volume thoroughly. No clue is given as to the identity of the new editor beyond the statement on the title page which describes Book I as:

> The *Grounds* and *Principles* of MUSICK/according to the *Gamut;* being newly Written,/and made more Easie for Young Practitioners,/according to the Method now in Practice,/by an Eminent Master in that *Science.//*

Leaving intact John Playford's Preface and his Essay ("Of Musick in General . . ."), the anonymous editor rewrote and reorganized almost all else. He omitted the elegy to Playford and transferred to the end of the volume the "Catalogue of Books" which had appeared in the twelfth edition. He totally revised and modernized Chapter I, including in it such passages as were relevant and up-to-date from Chapters II and III, and throwing out most of the old and cumbersome descriptions of the modal and hexachordal systems. For a new second chapter, he revised the former seventh chapter—a description of rhythmic values and divisions—following this, with the former ninth as third chapter, "Of the Moods, or Proportions of the Time or Measure of Notes."[22]

The former Chapter V, "Of Tuning the Voice," now shortened and improved, became Chapter IV. In turn, the former Chapter VIII, "Of the Rests or Pauses, of Pricks or Points of Addition, and Notes of Syncopation,"[23] became Chapter V, while Chapter VI with its unvocal enharmonicism, was deleted.

For the new Chapter VI, the anonymous editor wrote a new section on musical notation (using material from Chapter X), clearing away much old and useless lumber. The very first sentence demonstrates the process:

---

22. The chapter was not ultraconservative. "Mood, Tune, and Prolation," as outlined by Morley, for instance, are stripped of ancient concepts and brought right up to date. The fact is, the editor really did not go into "Proportion" in the old, specialized *musical* sense at all, but treated it as a general term, in its modern sense.

23. Actually, this might more logically have come just after new Chapter III.

> The Principal Part of which Characters/are a *Flat* and a *Sharp;* the *Flat* is marked/thus ♭, and the *Sharp* thus *. . .

Eliminating the old concept according to which the ♭ and ♮ signs were regarded as "b cliffs" represented quite an important step forward for English theory; and so did the addition of chapters on keys[24] and ornaments. (Indeed these new chapters—numbers VII and VIII respectively—have seemed sufficiently valuable to include intact as Appendix I to this facsimile of the twelfth edition.)

Similar changes throughout the second book were equally effective in modernizing it. However, Purcell's version of the third book was left intact, except for the title, which lost the now unwarranted adjective "brief" to become, simply, "An Introduction to the Art of Descant: Or, Composing Musick in Parts. Book III. With the Additions of the late Mr. Henry Purcell." A few misprints such as the two on page ninety-one were corrected, *e.g.,* Figure "6," coinciding with the first beat in the penultimate bar in the example for Rule II, was changed to "8."

At the end of the thirteenth edition, a new advertisement for Henry Playford's wares appears, along with the following interesting note:

> By reason of the small Encouragement, and/for the more compleat Printing of that Excellent Ma-/ster, Mr. H. *Purcell's* Vocal and Instrumental Musick in/all their Parts,[25] a longer Time is given to all Subscribers,/ hoping by *Trinity-Term* next to meet with greater En-/couragement, so that Subscriptions will be taken till/then, and the Book deliver'd at the end of that Term:/Proposals are to be had at *H. Playford's* Shop; where/will be speedily publish'd, a Catalogue of all the *Musick/Books* sold at the same place, in which will be several/*Italian* Musick-Books, and some newly come over.//

24. *Of the several KEYS in Musick; also what/a Key is, and how to Name your Notes in/any of them.*

25. The instrumental works to which Playford refers here would be either Purcell's *Ayres for Theatre (A Collection of Ayres, Compos'd for the Theatre, and upon Other Occasions)* or his *Ten Sonata's in Four Parts,* or both, these being published that same year (*i.e.,* 1697). The vocal collection referred to undoubtedly was *Orpheus Britannicus,* Vol. I, which Playford did not manage to get through the press until the following year.

Though described on its title page as "Corrected and Enlarged," the fourteenth edition actually differs very little from the thirteenth. The "Short Ayres or Songs of Two Voices," last seen in the eleventh edition, were restored;[26] "Instructions for Divine Services" were reprinted; and various small musical additions were made. Otherwise the fourteenth edition, printed in the first year of the eighteenth century, modernized the appearance of the treatise by utilizing the new movable type and "tied-note" in "round notation" (*i.e.*, modern round-shaped notation with beamed stems for repetitive rhythmic values smaller than quarter notes).[27]

---

26. These have been included entire as Appendix II. Two other small additions to the fourteenth edition have also been included as Appendices III and IV for similar reasons. The first, *"Some TUNES of the most usual PSALMS, Broken* (*i.e.*, varied and ornamented) *for the VIOLIN,"* provides valuable insight into contemporary performance-practices; the second, comprising two new and interesting canons (*Venite* and *Laudate Deum*), justifies inclusion on musical grounds alone, even though the author (or authors) has not yet been identified. Apart from relieving some of the congestion resulting from crowding, the engraver of the new plates found nothing to change. He did, however, cut expenses by omitting music for second strophes.

27. Actually, Playford had used the "new ty'd note" as early as 1658, as L. M. Middleton observed in his article on Playford in the *Dictionary of National Biography.* John Hawkins also mentioned Playford's invention in his *A General History of the Science and Practice of Music* (London, Novello, 2nd ed., 1853), Volume II, p. 687, where in a footnote he explained that

> ... about the year 1660 Playford invented what he called the new tyed note, wherein by one or two strokes continued from the bottom of each note to the next, the quavers and semiquavers were formed into compages of four or six, as the time required, a contrivance that rendered the musical characters much more legible than before. The Dutch followed this example soon after the English had set it; and afterwards the French, and after them the Germans; but so lately as the year 1724, when Marcello's Psalms were published in a splendid edition at Venice, the Italians printed after the old manner, and so did the Spaniards till within these very few years.

The passage in question appears in Playford's unnumbered edition of 1658 on page thirty-one. It is short enough to be reproduced here entire:

Of the Tying of Notes.

Printed by William Pearson for Henry Playford, the fourteenth edition served as a precise model for all subsequent impressions. The last five editions differed from the fourteenth only in a few minor details, such as the correction in the fifteenth of 1703 of the misnumbering of all pages after page eighty caused by a skip to page ninety-one at that point. With the fourteenth edition, Playford's book had reached its final form and continued on only as a *vade mecum* that had outlived its essential purpose. The drying-up of England's native musical culture had undermined the general *raison d'être* for this specifically English musical handbook, which had developed, *mutatis mutandis,* according to the needs of a renascent tradition. As the eighteenth century began, those laboring in the shadow of the giant Handel —Avison, Buononcini, Geminiani, Prelleur, Tosi, *et al.*—soon pre-empted its domain with their own musical treatises.

Study of the consecutive editions of Playford's *Introduction* still may be considered useful to the modern musician in a number of ways. As an aid to the understanding of musical thought in seventeenth-century England, the treatise provides a series of chronologically exact check-points, useful for evaluating the development of English music and musicianship during the vital three-quarters of a century from 1653 to 1730. It thus affords valuable insights into the traditions of musical composition and performance—all helpful for critical evaluation of any given piece of music—and also tells us much about the learner's approach to his art in any particular decade. Careful attention to the development from edition to edition of various concepts and techniques, forms and media, yields, therefore, not only a sense of the manner in which new styles grew out of the old, but also provides, *pari passu,* an account of the advancing musical pedagogy experienced by each new generation of English musicians. No better key to the investigation of general stylistic development can be found than that provided by this book's history, nor can any clearer view be obtained of the various stages through which any young seventeenth-century musician gained mastery over his art.

This Example shews that many times in songs or Lessons, Two, or Foure, or more Quavers and Semiquavers are Tyed together by a long Stroke on the Top of their Tails: And though they be so, they are the same with the other, not differing in the Measure or Proportion of Time, neither by the Placing of the Tail of a Note up or down doe make any Alteration.

To examine the incredibly complicated solmization system still in use is thus both interesting and instructive. It is interesting because the system reveals that musical pedagogy in seventeenth-century England was only midway along in the transition from the modes and hexachords of the gamut to the tetrachords and heptads of the major–minor system. It is instructive because the keen modern student of seventeenth-century English music can do no better than to learn this whole system—*ad astra per aspera*—with the help of Playford's instructions.

For the music historian, it is also profitable to compare Playford's instructions with both earlier and later practical formulations. Understanding various relationships, such as that between ancient mutation and modern modulation, or knowing respective functions of the syllables "mi" and "ti," not only clarifies the tradition of Restoration music, it also gives us a new perspective on the music of our own times. Various modes of musical thought which have shaped the history of musical style from Purcell to Schoenberg are herein to be found.

Our understanding of Henry Purcell's art is increased by study of the early editions of the *Introduction,* since they no doubt provided him with material for musical study in his youth. Such understanding will be further enhanced by acquaintance with the twelfth edition of 1694, which he so meticulously and thoroughly revised. As might be expected from the modernistic tendencies revealed in his own music, Purcell's theoretical formulations reflect a lively interest in latest trends; but this interest stands side by side with a typically English faith in convention. Disregarding the advanced attitude toward use of unprepared dissonances demonstrated by Monteverdi and his followers nearly ninety years earlier, Purcell still held in 1694 that only the "false or defective fifth" did not require preparation.[28]

On the other hand, he did advocate free use of the latest harmonic combinations then in vogue among Italian composers. Such harmonies as those involving the "third and fourth together to introduce a close" (p. 132), the "sharp seventh . . . for Recitative songs," the flat seventh (p. 131), and the Neapolitan sixth (p. 132), show him to have been well in advance of most of his English contemporaries.

---

28. See facsimile, *infra* pp. 92—101, 130.

Similarly, Christopher Simpson (with whom Purcell took occasion for genteel dispute on page 115) still held in his theoretical treatise[29] to the old notion of the bass as groundwork for all musical composition, while Purcell went along with "modern authors," who suited their contrapuntal and harmonic inventions to the upper melody (see p. 101). He even went so far as to fashion the bass to the melody in composing "Fugues" (as he termed them, although we would not).[30] As may be seen throughout this section of the treatise (pp. 106–114), he used the bass as the imitating, later voice (*comes*) in almost all of his "Fugues," departing from this procedure only for old-fashioned polyphonic through-imitation, which he labeled "Reports or imitation."

It is significant in this regard that without remarking on it, Purcell took the trouble to rewrite many of the basses for the Psalm tunes. Once committed to a task, he spared himself no pains, as we know from his arrangements of melodies printed at the end of Book I (pp. 46–53), as well as from his contribution to Daniel Warner's *Psalm Book*[31] mentioned in the advertisements at the end of the Preface to the twelfth edition (p. 53).

In embracing modern Italian methods, Purcell endorsed a number of innovations which recur throughout the *Introduction.* Some, of course, are to be found in earlier versions. For instance, the essay on the "Italian manner of singing" beginning on page thirty-one harks back to the fourth edition, being taken, as we have seen, from Caccini's famed *Le Nuove Musiche* of 1601 by "an English Gentleman who had lived long in Italy, and being returned, Taught the same here." It cannot have been coincidental that he, like Caccini, should have named his master to have been the "famous *Scipione del Palla,*" nor that the examples he chose to print are taken straight out of Caccini's publication with no acknowledgment and no changes other than translation of the original Italian rubrics.[32]

29. *A Compendium of Practical Musick* (London, 1667), p. 29.

30. See Glossary for a contemporary definition of this term.

31. *A Collection of some Verses out of the Psalms of David*... composed in two parts... revised by Mr. Henry Purcell (London, E. Jones, 1694). Presumably this is the collection referred to above despite the slight difference in the titles. However, the *Whole Book of Psalms and Hymns... in three parts,* to which Purcell refers the reader at the bottom of page fifty-three, clearly is another collection.

32. [Giulio Caccini] LE NVOVE/MVSICHE/DI GIVLIO CACCINI/DETTO ROMANO/Musico del Serenissimi Gran Duca di Toscana./Noua-

Another important Italian influence upon English music was recognized by Purcell early in his career when he published his sonatas of 1683 "in Imitation of the most fam'd Italian Masters."[33] In the "Art of Descant," on page 125, he again emphasizes the importance of this Italianate form, "the chiefest Instrumental music now in request." His specific reference is to a short passage from Lelio Colista's Sonata No. IV in D major,[34] which he cites as a good example of "double descant" (p. 124).

Not only the style of composition of these sonatas, but the instrument for which they were written, the violin, was of Italian origin. In the special section of Playford's treatise which is devoted to this instrument, "A Brief Introduction to the Playing on the Treble-Violin," there is no mention of Italian influence. Even the tunes cited are English. The shortness of the bow, the manner of holding the instrument, and an actual statement (p. 77) indicate that French influence was perhaps as important as Italian.[35]

In the Third Book, "A Brief Introduction to the Art of Descant, or Composing Music in Parts," significant instances of Italian influence are frequent. Besides those referred to above,[36] Purcell

---

mente con somma diligenza reuiste, corrette, & ristampate./[Printer's device]/IN VENETIA,/[rule]/APPRESSO ALESSANDRO RAVERII,/ M.D.CII./(The modern facsimile edition: Rome, Reale Accademia d'Italia, 1934, reproduces the Marescotti edition of 1601.). It is perhaps even more interesting that the anonymous English gentleman should have copied the typographical mistake—for such it seems—which has obscured the identity of Scipione del Palma (*Die Musik in Geschichte und Gegenwart,* Vol II, col. 609) since that time. (See also *Grove's Dictionary,* 5th ed., Vol. II, p. 6, for other versions of his name: Scipione de' Vecchi or Scipione delle Palle.) This slip causes one to wonder if the "anonymous English gentleman" may have been a fictional personality, invented for promotional purposes, Italianism being so much in vogue then.

33. *Trio Sonatas* (Paris, L'Oiseau Lyre, *c.* 1936). The Preface is reproduced in facsimile.

34. Michael Tilmouth, "The Technique and Forms of Purcell's Sonatas," *Music & Letters,* Vol. XL, No. 2 (April, 1959), pp. 109–21. See also his edition of Colista's sonata (London, Stainer and Bell, 1960).

35. *Cf.* David Boyden, *The History of Violin Playing from its Origins to 1761* (London: Oxford University Press, 1965), pp. 210 and 245. Plate 22 shows the French style of playing the violin, which seems to be that described by Playford.

36. That mentioned in connection with Playford's tenth edition was deleted, although the musical example itself remained.

calls attention to a variety of elegant discords favored by Italian composers (pp. 131–133), and in the section on singing, includes a long "ayre" in recitative style which, as we have seen, originally appeared in Caccini's *Le Nuove Musiche.* Interestingly enough, it bears more than a faint melodic resemblance to the beginning of Monteverdi's *Cruda Amarilli,* a piece also to be seen in Purcell's own transcription for viols of Monteverdi's madrigal (which occasioned the famous polemic of G. M. Artusi)[37] with the undoubtedly derivative monodic setting[38] until recent times attributed to Pietro Reggio.

Indeed this little "ayre," *Deh, dove son fuggiti,* sums up the whole frustrating problem of dramatic recitative in England. Beginning early in the seventeenth century, numerous attempts were made in behalf of Italian opera to effect successful transplantation to England similar to that which had developed so naturally the madrigal tradition. William Davenant, Tom Killigrew, Nicholas Laniere, Henry Lawes, John Milton, Walter Porter, and many others tried but failed to establish native English opera. Even Purcell, whose *Dido and Aeneas* was uniquely successful among such attempts, found the declamatory flexibility and the impassioned freedom of Italian recitative style most difficult to duplicate on the English stage. The easy flow of harmonic progressions, the effective use of unprepared dissonance, and the eloquent but natural setting of the text—all qualities which may be observed even in second-rate Italian recitative, such as *Deh, dove son fuggiti*—Purcell did manage to imitate. Even so, then as always, the English language seems to have remained refractory in some essential way to the subtle shifts from lyric vocability to staccato declamation, and especially, as Playford's anonymous gentleman puts it on page forty-one, to "Exclamation without measure, as it were Talking in Harmony, and neglecting the Musick." With significantly rare exceptions, such as the

---

37. G. M. Artusi, *L'Artusi, ovvero, Delle imperfezioni della moderna musica* (Venice, 1600). The "Second Discourse," which discusses Monteverdi's piece and cites nine offending passages from it, is available in translation in Oliver Strunk's *Source Readings in Music History* (New York, Norton, 1950), pp. 393–404.

38. See F. B. Zimmerman, "Musical Borrowings in the English Baroque," *The Musical Quarterly,* Vol. LII, No. 4 (Oct., 1966), pp. 483–495. See also the article by Pamela J. Willets ["A Neglected Source of Monody and Madrigal," *Music & Letters,* Vol. XLIII, No. 4 (Oct., 1962), pp. 329—339], which clarifies the problem of attribution with regard to this piece.

recitative passages in Purcell's "From rosy bow'rs," successful application of these techniques eluded English composers, no matter how many attempts were made to introduce them into the mainstream of the English musical tradition.

Despite all such influence, successful or otherwise, seventeenth-century musical traditions remained essentially "English." Italian and French influences either were absorbed and naturalized, or fell by the wayside. Thus in studying English music history one should always distinguish between alleged or apparent influences, frequently either superficial, ephemeral, or both, and those which may be proved to have been genuinely effective. Borrowed techniques did not often take root, and though perhaps vaguely influential, cannot often be traced clearly into the mainstream of English music, which tended to retain its native character even during periods of extensive assimilation from abroad up to the time of the so-called Italian invasion at the end of the seventeenth century.[39]

That English musical traditions themselves supplied the main forces and materials to shape future development is particularly evident in all three books of the twelfth edition of *An Introduction to the Skill of Musick.* Playford made a good case for this notion at the outset, in the last few paragraphs of the essay, "Of music in general, its divine and civil uses," his case being strengthened throughout by frequent reference to English musical institutions and customs.[40] But of all the evidence contained in the various parts of the *Introduction* which might be adduced to substantiate this notion of the permanence of native English traits, that reflecting Purcell's own musical personality is most persuasive. Indeed, from his contribution to the twelfth edition of Playford's *Introduction,* we gain a fresh view of this Restoration genius, this *Orpheus Britannicus,* whose lifework fulfills, even as it transcends, the musical ideals of Restoration England.

Musically, the late seventeenth century was a time of prodigious effort and achievement in England. The contrast between the barrenness of musical life in London in 1654, when the first edition of the *Introduction* appeared, and its fruitful activity within the sev-

---

39. For full discussion of this matter, see the author's "Features of Italian Style in Elizabethan Part-Songs and Madrigals." (Unpublished B.Litt. Thesis, Oxford, 1955.)

40. See pp. 00 to 00 below.

eral spheres of court, chamber, church, theater, and public concert hall in 1694 is enough to show *how* prodigious. The chief figure—"the greatest genius England ever had," as Roger North put it—was Purcell himself. The very fact that he took on so formidable a task as that of reediting Playford's *Introduction* is revealing.

By 1694, when his health very likely already was failing, Purcell was incredibly busy composing for the stage, for Westminster Abbey, for Royal chamber music performances, for various celebrations, and for public concerts. During the year, he prepared several pieces of music for Queen Mary's funeral, in addition to composing "Come ye sons of Art away," the annual birthday ode to the Queen. For other ceremonial occasions, he wrote a New Year's ode (setting Matthew Prior's "Hymn to the Sun," now lost), an ode ("Great parent, hail") for a centennial celebration at Trinity College, Dublin, and the magnificent *Te Deum* and *Jubilate* for the celebration of St. Cecilia's Day at St. Paul's, London. Above and beyond all this, he set eight songs, composed an impressive anthem ("The way of God"), and provided incidental music for seven theatrical productions. And he also carried forward his responsibilities as organist at the Abbey, as harpsichord repairer for the Royal court, and as a frequent performer before audiences in court and city. Pressed as he must have been by so many duties, his willingness to edit the *Introduction* seems in retrospect an act of courage, perhaps even of foolhardiness.

Characteristically, he approached the task without fussiness, but with meticulous attention to detail. The tendency toward straightforwardness and simplicity in the *Introduction,* already noted in Playford's tenth edition and elsewhere, is even more clearly manifest here, and also more directly parallel to contemporary trends in harmonic and contrapuntal expression in England, just then rather belatedly becoming less and less encumbered by the confusion inherent in antiquated polyphonic writing.

Initially, in the first dozen pages, the student is taken briskly but thoroughly through various kinds of contrapuntal motion, intervallic usage, dissonance treatment, and cadential techniques. Then, after discussing "allowed" and "disallowed" parallel motion, Purcell introduced a comparative example (p. 101), demonstrating at the same time a fresh approach by composing a bass to a treble, rather than the reverse, which was then customary. The significance of this new departure lay not only in the reversal of the technique of composing *from* the bass—itself a fairly recent reaction in England to composition from the tenor—but in the emphasis it placed upon the invention of a melodious bass line, and on the polarity and equal importance of upper and lower melodies. Purcell made the most of his matter, leading the student meticulously, step by step through all the reasoning involved.[41] (For thoroughness his method may be compared to that of Schoenberg in the *Harmonielehre* of 1911.) Purcell left nothing to chance in showing prospective pupils how to write "a formal or regular bass to a treble" (p. 105).

His exposition of the techniques "Of Fuge, or Pointing" is, from the historical as well as the pedagogical view, even more important. As Alfred Mann has explained,[42] Purcell not only established a clear distinction between Imitation (or "reports") and a harmonically based fugal technique a third of a century before Rameau's *Traité de l'harmonie,* he also clearly recognized that the fugue was a tonal procedure,[43] not a technical form. He was one of the earliest composers clearly to see beyond the technical side of fugal imitation into the harmonic era, when tunefulness and tonal structure would outweigh the criteria of elegant polyphony. Again with meticulous thoroughness, Purcell went through all eight varieties of "fuguing," from simple two-part writing to the strictest and most complex canonic techniques for four and five voices. It is characteristic both of his basic loyalty to English tradition and of his unegotistical outlook that for canonic paradigms he chose not his own works but those of other English composers, whom he cited with unstinting praise, speaking of "the wonderful variety" in Elway Bevin's book of canons (p. 114), and of John Blow's canon "Four in One: Glory be to the Father" as "enough to recommend him for one of the Greatest Masters in the World" (p. 141).

While differing with one small point in Christopher Simpson's *Compendium of Music,* he praised it as the "most Ingenious Book" he knew on the subject. The difference, though slight, is important (see p. 115). Holding Simpson's example as "too strict and destructive to good Air, which ought to be preferred before such nice

41. See pp. 101–106.

42. *The Study of Fugue* (New Brunswick, Rutgers University Press, 1958), pp. 46–48, 50.

43. See also Imogene Horsley, *Fugue: History and Practice* (New York: The Free Press, 1966), p. 81, where Purcell and Simpson are singled out as the only composer-theorists in seventeenth-century England to recognize the tonal answer.

Rules," he again emphasized his ideal for melodic beauty—a productive ideal, indeed, in view of the abundance he created. Revising Simpson's example, Purcell demonstrated at a stroke not only his gift for achieving simple and natural melodic beauty, but also the gist of the new harmonic ideals which the Baroque had brought into being.

With Purcell, however, it was not a matter of contest between melodic invention and harmonic ingenuity, but rather a synthesis of these two faculties. As both student of and contributor to the musical wisdom residing in Playford's little handbook, he could no more clearly have symbolized at once both the unique strength and the tragic flaw inherent in native English music, which very soon was to be overwhelmed by an influx of music and musicians from Italy and other foreign lands.

Lexington, Kentucky
September, 1967

FRANKLIN B. ZIMMERMAN

1972

D. Loggan sculp.
IOHANNIS
PLAYFORD

AN

INTRODUCTION

TO THE

Skill of Musick,

IN THREE BOOKS.

THE FIRST CONTAINS

The *Grounds* and *Rules* of MUSICK, according to the *Gam-ut*, and other *Principles* thereof.

THE SECOND,

INSTRUCTIONS and *LESSONS* both for the *Bass-Viol* and *Treble-Violin.*

THE THIRD,

The ART of *DESCANT*, or Composing *Musick* in Parts: In a more Plain and Easie Method than any heretofore Published.

By JOHN PLAYFORD.

The Twelfth Edition.

Corrected and Amended by Mr. Henry Purcell.

In the SAVOY, Printed by E. *Jones*, for *Henry Playford* at his Shop near the *Temple* Church. 1694.

A

PREFACE

TO ALL

Lovers of Musick.

MUSICK in ancient Times was held in as great Estimation, Reverence, and Honour, by the most Noble and Virtuous Persons, as any of the Liberal Sciences whatsoever, for the manifold Uses thereof, conducing to the Life of Man. Philosophers accounted it an Invention of the Gods, bestowing it on Men to make them better condition'd than bare Nature afforded, and conclude a special necessity thereof in the Education of Children; partly from its natural Delight, and partly from the Efficacy it hath in moving the Affections to Virtue; comprehending chiefly these three Arts in the Education of Youth, *Grammar*, *Musick*, and *Gymnastic*; this last is for the Exercise of their Limbs. *Quintilian* reports, in his time the same Men taught both *Grammar* and *Musick*. Those then who intend the Practice thereof, must allow *Musick* to be the Gift of God; yet (like other his Graces and Benefits) it is not given to the Idle, but they must reach it with the Hand of Industry, by putting in Practice the *Works* and *Inventions* of skilful Artists; for meerly to Speak and Sing are of Nature, and this double use of the Ar-

ticulate

ticulate *Voice* the rudeſt Swains of all Nations do make; but to Speak well, and Sing well, are of Art: Therefore when I had conſidered the great want of Books, ſetting forth the Rules and Grounds of this Divine Science of *Muſick* in our own Language, it was a great Motive with me to undertake this Work, though I muſt confeſs, our Nation is at this time plentifully ſtor'd with skilful Men in this Science, better able than my ſelf to have undertaken this Work; but their ſlowneſs and modeſty (being, as I conceive, unwilling to appear in Print about ſo ſmall a matter,) has made me adventure on it, though with the danger of not being ſo well done as they might have perform'd it: And I was the rather induc'd thereunto, for that the Preſcription of Rules of all Arts and Sciences ought to be deliver'd in plain and brief Language, and not in Flowers of Eloquence; which Maxim I have follow'd: For after the moſt brief, plain and eaſie Method I could invent, I have here ſet down the *Grounds* of *Muſick*, omitting nothing in this Art which I conceiv'd neceſſary for the Practice of Young Beginners, both for Vocal and Inſtrumental *Muſick.* Alſo I have in a brief Method ſet forth the Art of Compoſing *Two*, *Three*, and *Four Parts* Muſically, in ſuch eaſie and plain Rules as are moſt neceſſary to be underſtood by Young Practitioners. The Work as it is, I muſt confeſs, is not all my own, ſome part thereof being Collected out of other Authors which have written on this Subject, the which I hope will make it more approv'd.

J. Playford.

Of Musick in General, and of its *Divine* and *Civil Uses*.

MUSICK *is an Art Unsearchable, Divine, and Excellent, by which a true Concordance of Sounds or Harmony is produced, that rejoyceth and cheareth the Hearts of Men; and hath in all Ages and in all Countries been highly reverenc'd and esteem'd; by the* Jews *for Religion and Divine Worship in the Service of God, as appears by Scripture; by the* Grecians *and* Romans *to induce Virtue and Gravity, and to incite to Courage and Valor. Great Disputes were among* Ethnick *Authors about the first Inventor, some for* Orpheus, *some* Linus, *both famous Poets and Musicians; others for* Amphion, *whose Musick drew Stones to the building of the Walls of* Thebes; *as* Orpheus *had, by the harmonious Touch of his Harp, moved the wild Beasts and Trees to dance: But the true meaning thereof is, That by virtue of their Musick, and their wise and pleasing Musical Poems, the one brought the Savage and Beast-like* Thracians *to Humanity and Gentleness; the other perswaded the rude and careless* Thebans *to the fortifying of their City, and to a Civil Conversation: The* Egyptians *to* Apollo, *attributing the first Invention of the Harp to him; and certainly they had an high esteem of the Excellency of Musick, to make* Apollo *(who was the God of Wisdom) to be the God of Musick: But the People of God do truly acknowledge a far more ancient Inventor of this Divine Art,* Jubal *the*

sixth

sixth from Adam, *who, as it is recorded,* Gen. 4.27. was the Father of all that handle the Harp or Organ. *St.* Augustine *goeth yet farther, shewing that it is the Gift of God himself, and a Representation or Admonition of the sweet Consent and Harmony which his Wisdom hath made in the Creation and Administration of the World. And well it may be term'd a Divine and Mysterious Art, for among all those rare Arts and Sciences, with which God hath endued Men, this of* Musick *is the most sublime and excellent for its wonderful Effects and Inventions: It hath been the study of Millions of Men for many thousand years, yet none ever attain'd the full scope and perfection thereof, but still appear'd new Matter for their Inventions; and, which is most wonderful, the whole Mystery of this Art is comprised in the compass of three Notes or Sounds, which is most ingeniously observ'd by Mr.* Christopher Simpson, *in his* Division-Violist, *p.* 18. *in these words:* All Sounds that can possibly be joyn'd at once together in Musical Concordance, are still but the reiterated Harmony in *Three*; a significant Emblem of that Supreme and Incomprehensible Trinity, *Three in One*, Governing and Disposing the whole Machine of the World, with all its included Parts in a perfect Harmony; for in the Harmony of Sounds, there is some great and hidden Mystery above what hath been yet discovered. *And Mrs.* Catherine Philips, *in her Encomium on Mr.* Henry Laws *his Second Book of* Ayres, *hath these words:*

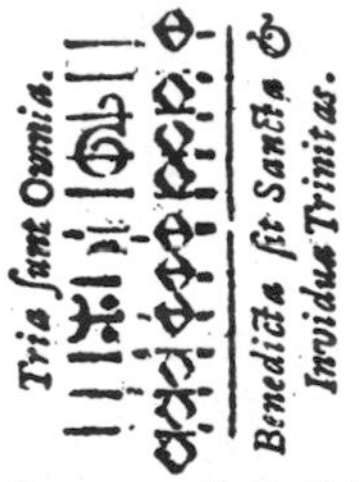
Tria sunt Omnia.
Benedicta sit Sancta
Individua Trinitas.

Nature, which in the vast Creation's Soul,
That steady curious Agent in the whole,

The

The Art of Heaven, the order of this Frame,
Is only *Musick* in another Name.
And as ſome King, conqu'ring what was his own,
Hath choice of ſeveral Titles to his Crown;
So *Harmony* on this ſcore now, that then,
Yet ſtill is all that takes and governs Men.
Beauty is but *Compoſure*, and we find
Content is but the *Concord* of the Mind;
Friendſhip the *Uniſon* of well-tun'd Hearts;
Honour's the *Chorus* of the Nobleſt Parts:
And all the World, on which we can reflect,
Muſick to th' Ear, or to the Intellect.

Nor hath there yet been any Reaſon given of that ſympathy in Sounds, that the Strings of a Viol *being ſtruck, and another* Viol *laid at a diſtance, and tuned in concordance to it, the ſame Strings thereof ſhould ſound and move in a ſympathy with the other, tho' not touch'd: Nor that the Sound of a* Sackbut *or* Trumpet *ſhould, by a ſtronger emiſſion of Breath, skip from* Concord *to* Concord, *before you can force it into any gradation of Tones or Notes.* Ath. Kercherus, *a Learned Writer, reports, That in* Calabria, *and other Parts of* Italy, *there is a poiſonous Spider called the* Tarantula, *by which ſuch as are bitten fall into a frenzy of Madneſs and Laughter; to allay the immoderate Paſſion thereof,* Muſick *is the ſpeedy Remedy and Cure, for which they have ſolemn Songs and Tunes.*

The firſt and chief Uſe of Muſick *is for the Service and Praiſe of* God, *whoſe Gift it is. The ſecond Uſe is for the Solace of Men, which as it is agreeable unto Nature, ſo it is allowed by God, as a temporal Bleſſing to recreate and cheer Men after long ſtudy and weary labour in their Vocations.* Eccl.40.20. Wine and Muſick rejoyce the Heart: *as the Philoſopher adviſeth,* Muſica Medicina eſt moleſtiæ illius per labores ſuſcipitur.

Ælia-

Ælianus *in his* Hist. Animal. l. 10. c. 29. *writeth, That of all Beasts, there is none that is not delighted with Harmony, but only the Ass.* H. Stephanus *reports, That he say a Lion in* London *leave his Meat to hear Musick. Myself, as I travelled some years since near* Royston, *met an Herd of Stags, about 20, upon the Road, following a Bagpipe and Violin, which while the Musick play'd they went forward; when it ceas'd, they all stood still; and in this manner they were brought out of* Yorkshire *to* Hampton-Court. *If irrational Creatures so naturally love, and are delighted with Musick, shall not rational Man, who is endued with the knowledge thereof? A Learned Author hath this Observation, That Musick is used only of the most Aerial Creatures, lov'd and understood by Man: The Birds of the Air, those pretty winged Choristers, how at the approach of the Day do they warble forth their Maker's Praise? Among which, observe the little Lark, who by a Natural Instinct doth very often mount up the Sky as high as his Wings will bear him, and there warble out his Melody as long as his strength enables him, and then descends to his Flock, who presently send up another Chorister to supply this Divine Service. It is also observed of the Cock, which* Chaucer *calls* Chanticleer, *his Crowing is sounded Musically, and doth allude to the perfect Syllables of the word* Hal-le-lu-jah.

Ath. Kircher *writes also, That the Cock doth sound a perfect* Eight *Musically, thus, when his Hens come from their Nest.*

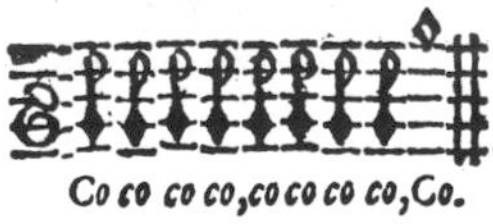
Co co co co, co co co co, Co.

He hath several other Observations of Sounds by such Animals. The Philosopher says, Not to be Animum Musicum, *is not to be* Animal Rationale. *And the*

the Italian *Proverb is*, God loves not him, whom he hath not made to love Musick. *Nor doth Musick only delight the Mind of Man, and Beasts and Birds, but also conduceth much to bodily health by the exercise of the Voice in Song, which doth clear and strengthen the Lungs, and if to it be joyn'd the Exercise of the Limbs, none need fear* Asthma *or Consumption; the want of which Exercise is often the death of many Students: Also much benefit hath been found thereby, by such as have been troubled with defects in Speech, as Stammering and bad Utterance. It gently breaths and vents the Mourners Grief, and heightens the Joys of them that are cheerful: It abateth Spleen and Hatred. The valiant Soldier in Fight is animated when he hears the sound of the Trumpet, the Fife and Drum: All Mechanick Artists do find it chear them in their weary Labours.* Scaliger (Exerc. 302.) *gives a reason of these Effects, because the Spirits about the heart taking in that trembling and dancing Air in the body, are moved together, and stir'd up with it; or that the Mind, harmonically composed, is roused up at the Tunes of the Musick. And farther, we see even young Babes are charm'd asleep by their Singing Nurses; nay, the poor labouring Beasts at Plow and Cart are chear'd by the sound of Musick, thô it be but their Masters Whistle. If God then hath granted such benefit to Men by the Civil Exercise, sure the Heavenly and Divine Use will much more redound to our eternal Comfort; if with our Voices we joyn our Hearts when we sing in his holy Place. Venerable* Bede *writeth, That no Science but* Musick *may enter the Doors of the Church: The Use of which in the Worship and Service of God, that it hath been anciently used, and should still be continued, may be easily proved from the Evidence of God's Word, and the Practice of the Church*

in

in all Ages: You ſhall ſeldom meet Holy David *without an Inſtrument in his Hand, and a Pſalm in his Mouth; Fifty three Holy Metres or Pſalms be dedicated to his Chief Muſician* Jeduthun, *to compoſe Muſick to them: He was one in whom the Spirit of God delighted to dwell, for no Evil Spirit will abide to tarry where* Muſick *and Harmony are lodg'd; for when he play'd before* Saul, *the Evil Spirit departed immediately. This power of* Muſick *againſt Evil Spirits,* Luther *ſeemeth to think that it doth ſtill remain,* Scimus *(ſaith he)* Muſicam Dæmonibus etiam inviſam & intolerabilem eſſe, *We know that* Muſick *is moſt dreadful and intolerable to the Devils. How acceptable Divine Harmony was to God in his worſhip, appears in* 2 Chron. 5. 12, 13. Alſo the *Levites,* which were the Singers, all of them of *Aſaph,* of *Heman,* of *Jeduthun,* with their Sons and their Brethren, being arrayed in white Linen, having Cymbals, and Pſalteries, and Harps, ſtood at the Eaſt end of the Altar, and with them an hundred and twenty Prieſts ſounding with Trumpets: It came even to paſs, as the Trumpeters and Singers were as one, to make one ſound to be heard in praiſing and thanking the Lord; And when they lift up their Voice with the Trumpets and Cymbals, and Inſtruments of Muſick, *&c.* that then the Houſe was filled with a Cloud, even the Houſe of the Lord. *The Uſe of Muſick was continued in the Church of the* Jews, *even until the Deſtruction of their Temple and Nation by* Titus *And the uſe thereof alſo began in the* Chriſtian *Church in our Saviour and his Apoſtles time. If you conſult the Writings of the Primitive Fathers, you ſhall ſcarce meet with one that doth not write of the Divine Uſe of* Muſick *in Churches; and yet true it is, that*

ſome

ſome of them did find fault with ſome Abuſes thereof in the Service of God; (and ſo they would now if they were alive;) but that condemneth the right Uſe thereof no more than the Holy Supper is condemned by St. Paul, *while he blameth thoſe who ſhamefully profaned it. The Chriſtian Emperors, Kings, and Princes in all Ages, have had this Divine Science in great Eſteem and Honour:* Conſtantine *the Great, and* Theodoſius, *did both of them begin and ſing Divine Hymns in the Chriſtian Congregations; and* Juſtinian *the Emperor compoſed an Hymn to be ſung in the Church, which began,* To the only begotten Son and Word of God. *Of* Charles *the Great it is reported, That he went often into the Pſalmody and ſung himſelf, and appointed his Sons and other Princes what Pſalms and Hymns ſhould be ſung. But to come nearer home, Hiſtory tells us, That the ancient* Britains *of this Iſland had Muſicians before they had Books; and the* Romans, *that Invaded them, (who were not too forward to magnifie other Nations) confeſs what Power the* Druids *and* Bards *had over the People's Affections, by recording in Songs the Deeds of Heroick Spirits, their Laws and Religion being ſung in Tunes, and ſo without Letters tranſmitted to Poſterity; wherein they were ſo dextrous, that their Neighbours of* Gaul *came hither to learn it.* Alfred, *a* Saxon *King of this Land, was well skill'd in all manner of Learning, but in the knowledge of Muſick took moſt delight. King* Henry *the Eighth did much advance Muſick in the firſt part of his Reign, when his mind was more intent upon Arts and Sciences, at which time he invited the beſt Maſters out of* Italy, *and other Countries, whereby he grew to great Knowledge therein; of which he gave Teſtimony, by Compoſing with his own hand two entire*

Ser-

Services of five and six Parts, as it is Recorded by the Lord Herbert, *who writ his Life.* Edward *the Sixth was a Lover and Encourager thereof, if we may believe Dr.* Tye, *one of his Chapel, who put the* Acts of the Apostles *into Metre, and Composed the same to be sung in four Parts, which he printed and dedicated to the King: His Epistle began thus;*

Considering well, most Godly King,
 The Zeal and perfect Love
Your Grace doth bear to each good Thing,
 That given is from Above:
That such good Things your Grace might move,
 Your Lute when you assay,
In stead of Songs of Wanton Love,
 These Stories then to Play.

Queen Elizabeth *was not only a Lover of this Divine Science, but a good Proficient herein; and I have been informed by an ancient Musician, and her Servant, that she did often recreate herself on an excellent Instrument called the* Poliphant, *not much unlike a* Lute, *but strung with Wire: And that it was Her Care to Promote the same in the Worship of God, may appear by her 49th* Injunction. *And K.* James I. *granted his Letters Patents to the Musicians in* London *for a Corporation.*

Nor was his late Sacred Majesty, and blessed Martyr, King Charles *the First, behind any of his Predecessors in the love and promotion of this Science, especially in the Service of Almighty God, which with much Zeal he would hear reverently performed; and often appointed the Service and Anthems himself, especially that sharp Service Composed by Dr.* William Child, *being by his Knowledge in Musick a competent Judge therein, and could play his Part exactly well on the* Bass-Viol, *especially of those Incomparable Phantasies of Mr.* Coperario *to the* Organ.

Of

Of whose Virtues and Piety (by the infinite Mercy of Almighty God) this Kingdom lately enjoy'd a living Example in his Son King Charles *the Second, whose Love of this Divine Art appear'd by his Encouragement of it, and the Professors thereof, especially in his bountiful Augmentation of the Annual Allowance of the Gentlemen of His Chapel; which Example, if it were followed by the Superiors of our Cathedrals in this Kingdom, it would much encourage Men of this Art (who are there employed to Sing Praises to Almighty God) to be more studious in that Duty, aud would take off that Contempt which is cast upon many of them for their mean Performances and Poverty; but it is their and all true Christians sorrow, to see how that Divine Worship is contemned by blind Zealots, who does not, nor will not, understand the Use and Excellency thereof.*

But Musick *in this Age (like other Arts and Sciences) is in low esteem with the generality of People, our late and Solemn Musick, both Vocal and Instrumental, is now justled out of Esteem by the New Corants and Jiggs of Foreigners, to the Grief of all sober and judicious Understanders of that formerly solid and good Musick: Nor must we expect Harmony in Peoples Minds, so long as Pride, Vanity, Faction, and Discords, are so predominant in their Lives. But I conclude with the Words of Mr.* Owen Feltham *in his Resolves;* We find, *saith he,* that in Heaven there is *Musick* and *Hallelujahs* Sung; I believe it is an helper both to Good and Evil, and will therefore honour it when it *moves* to *Virtue*, and shall beware of it when it would *flatter* into *Vice*.

J. Playford.

On the DEATH of

Mr. JOHN PLAYFORD,

THE

Author *of These, and several other excellent WORKS.*

WE must submit, in vain with anxious Strife
We labour to support this load of Life;
No Prayers nor Penitence, no Tears prevail
With the Grim Tyrant of this mournful Vale.
Like Slaves in Amphitheatres of old,
Each others ghastly Ruin we behold.
And the Proud Sovereign, whom in the Morn
Imperial Crowns and Purple Robes adorn,
Drops from his glitt'ring Throne; e're mid of Day
Himself become the greedy Monster's Prey.
To the dark Shades so many ways we fly,
'Tis more a Miracle to be *Born*, than *Dye*.
And since our Course is by the Fates decreed,
He Runs it best who runs with swiftest speed.
Breathless and tir'd, the Wretch who lags behind,
Spurs on a jaded Life that's Lame and Blind:
And what avails one sad and painful Hour,
Whom Death's insatiate Jaws the next devour.

 So

So frail's our State, every mean Shrub we ſee
Has greater Strength and Permanence than we.
Though ſet in Tears to night, next morn' the Sun
Does his Eternal Race of Glory run.
The rolling Sand glides through the narrow ſpace,
And Age to Age renews the meaſur'd Chace.
Our brittle Glaſs, thin blown, and weakly burn'd,
Drops its ſhort Hour, and never more is turn'd.

Oh never more (*my Friend*) muſt my charm'd Ear
Thy chearful Voice, and skilful Muſick hear!
For ever ſilent is that Tuneful *Lyre*,
Which Men, in ſtead of Beaſts, did long inſpire.
And ſure the Dying Prince lamented well,
Not when the Emperor, but *Muſician*, fell.
When *Playford*'s hand the well-ſtrung Harp adorn'd,
The Principle of Life and Senſe we ſcorn'd;
Pleas'd with the Sound, we wiſh'd our Vital Air
Might only enter at the raviſh'd Ear.
Thoſe Glorious Deeds which were in Times of old
Of the Great *Thracean* fabulouſly told;
Or what's aſcrib'd to ſweet *Amphion*'s Name,
Was nobly done by this Great *Son* of *Fame*.
As high to Heav'n as Human Wings can ſpread,
And deep to Hell as Mortal Steps can tread,
His Pow'rful Strains with Learned Force did go,
Soar'd to the Skies, and pierc'd the Shades below.
His wond'rous Skill did Wealthy Fabricks raiſe,
Fair *Albion*'s liſt'ning Stones obey'd his Lays,
And ſtand the Signs of *Gratitude* and *Praiſe*.
All Sons of Art adorn'd their Rev'rend *Sire*,
And made his *Manſion* a Perpetual Quire.

His

His Life (Harmonious, Gentile, and Sweet,)
Was well compos'd, and in true Concord ſet.
Each Noble Part adorn'd its proper place,
And Rigid Virtue play'd the *Thorow-Baſs.*
Well he conſider'd that his tender *Lyre*
Muſt ſoon be broke, and Tuneful Breath expire;
And therefore with a Pious Care reſign'd
Theſe *Learned Monuments* he left behind.
With ſuch deploring Obſequies he fell,
As fetch'd the Fair *Euridice* from Hell.
But all in vain we mourn, while from our Eyes
Ev'ry belov'd and beauteous Object flies.
Ye Sons of Earth, whom proud Achievements ſwell,
Behold his Corps, and boaſt no more your Skill!
When all your Labour with Perfection's Crown'd,
Diſcord and *Death* ſucceed the ſweeteſt Sound.

The

The Contents of the First Book.

The Contents of the Second Book.

The Contents of the Third Book.

A Ca-

A Catalogue of Vocal and Instrumental MUSICK, *most of which are newly Reprinted for* H.Playford *at his Shop near the* Temple *Church.*

HArmonia Sacra, the first and second Books, being a Collection of *Divine Hymns* and *Dialogues:* Set to Musick by Dr. *Blow*, Mr. *H. Purcell*, and other Eminent Masters. *Cantica Sacra*, the first and second Books, being Anthems in 3 and 4 Parts in *Latin* and *English*. The *Psalms* to Musick in 4 Parts, in Folio. Four Choice Books of *Ayres* and *Dialogues*. Four Books of the *Theatre of Musick*. Six Books of the *Banquet of Musick*. The first and second Books of *Catches*.

Two Books for the *Virginals* or *Harpsichord*. The first and second Books of *Apollo*'s *Banquet*; being Collections of the newest Tunes for the *Treble-Violin*. The first and second Parts of the *Division-Violin*, containing the newest Grounds for the *Violin*. Mr. *Farmer*'s two *Consorts of Musick*, in 4 Parts. A *Consort of Musick* in 3 Parts, by Mr. *J. Lenton*, and Mr. *T. Tollet*. The *Dancing-Master*, with Tunes to each *Dance*, and Directions for *Country-Dancing*; the 8th Edition. A *Table* Engraven on *Copper*, shewing any *Note* within the compass of the *Bass-Viol*; very Beneficial for Young Practitioners on that Instrument.

☞ Also all sorts of *Ruled Paper* and *Ruled Books*, with *Songs* and *Tunes* fairly Prick'd, and Books on all other Subjects, are sold at the same Place.

☞ There will be speedily Printed for the Use of Mr. *D. Warner*'s Scholars, *A Collection of Part of the* PSALMS *of* DAVID, *and the Proper Tune to each Psalm*; *With* Instructions *at the end of the Preface for Singing of them.* Which will be sold by *Henry Playford*, and *D. Warner* aforesaid.

A N

AN INTRODUCTION TO THE Skill of Musick.

CHAP. I.
Of the Scale of Musick called the Gam-ut.

THE *Gam-ut* is the Ground of all *Musick*, *Vocal* or *Instrumental*, and (as *Ornithoparcus* reports) was composed by *Guido Aretinus*, about the Year 960, out of six Syllables in the Saphick of the Hymn of St. *Johan. Baptista*.

UT—*queant laxis* *REsonare fibris*
MIra gestorum *FAmuli tuorum*,
SOLve poluti *LAbii reatum*.

By another thus:

UT RE*livet* MI*serum* FA*tum* SOL*itúmq*; LA*borem*.

Ascending thus:

Ut Re Mi Fa Sol La. Ut Re. Sol La.

These

Theſe ſix Notes were uſed for many Years paſt in this order *Aſcending* and *Deſcending*, but now four are only in uſe, *viz.* *Sol*, *La*, *Mi*, *Fa*, (ſo that Ut and Re are changed into *Sol* and *La*) which are ſufficient to expreſs the ſeveral Sounds, and are leſs burthenſom to the Practitioner's Memory.

Example.

Sol La Mi Fa Sol La Fa Sol.

Beſides the Names of theſe Notes, there is uſed in our *Scale* of *Muſick*, called the *Gam-ut*, ſeven Letters of the *Alphabet*, which are ſet in the firſt Column, at the beginning of each Rule and Space, as G, *A*, *B*, *C*, *D*, *E*, *F*. And of theſe, there are three Septenaries aſcending one above the other, *G* being the firſt, agreeing with the third Letter in the *Greek* Alphabet called *Gamma*, and is made thus in *Greek* Γ, in *Engliſh* G, (the firſt Derivation thereof being from the ancient *Greeks*) as you may ſee in the *Scale* of *Muſick* at the end of this Chapter.

Theſe ſeven Letters are called *Cliffs*, or more properly *Cleaves*; and the Syllables adjoyning to them are the *Names* of the *Notes*. By the three Septenaries, are diſtinguiſh'd the three ſeveral *Parts* of *Muſick* into which the Scale is divided; Firſt, the *Baſſus*, which is the loweſt Part; Secondly, the *Mean*, or middle Part; and Thirdly, the *Treble*, or higheſt Part; ſo that according to theſe three Septenaries, *Gam-ut* is the loweſt Note, and *E la* the higheſt. And theſe, the uſual *Gam-uts* in Mr. *Morley*, and others, did not exceed; but there are many *Notes* uſed, both above and below, and

and do exceed this Compaſs both in *Vocal* and *Inſtrumental Muſick*, which ought not to be omited; for the Compaſs of Muſick is not confined: And tho' there be but three Septenaries of Notes in the Example of the *Gam-ut*, which amount to the compaſs of One and twenty Notes or Sounds; yet in the *Treble* or higheſt Part, as occaſion requires, you may *Aſcend* more Notes, for it is the ſame over again, only eight Notes higher: Or in your *Baſſus* or loweſt Part, you may *Deſcend* the like Notes lower than *Gam-ut*, as the compaſs of Voice or Inſtrument is able to extend, which will be the ſame, only *Eights* to thoſe above. And theſe Notes of *Addition* are uſually thus diſtinguiſhed:

Thoſe above *E la* in the *Treble* are called *Notes in Alt*, as *F fa ut in Alt*, *G ſol re ut in Alt*, &c. and thoſe below *Gam-ut* in the *Baſſus* are called *Double Notes*, as *Double F fa ut*, *Double E la mi*, &c. as being *Eights* or *Diapaſons* to thoſe above *Gam-ut*. I have therefore in the Table of the *Gam-ut* in this Book expreſſed them with double Letters in their right places.

The *Gam-ut* is drawn upon fourteen *Rules* and their *Spaces*, and comprehends all Notes or Sounds uſual in *Muſick*, either *Vocal* or *Inſtrumental*; yet when any of the Parts into which it is divided, *viz.* *Treble*, *Mean*, or *Tenor* and *Baſs*, ſhall come to be prick'd out by it ſelf in *Songs* or *Leſſons*, either for *Voice* or *Inſtrument*, *five Lines* is only uſual for one of thoſe Parts, as being ſufficient to contain the compaſs of *Notes* thereto belonging. And if there be any *Notes* that extend higher or lower, it is uſual to add a *Line* in that place with a Pen.

But for all *Leſſons* for the *Organ*, *Virginals*, or *Harp*, two Staves of *ſix Lines* together are required, one for the left hand or *lower Keys*, the other for the right hand or *upper Keys*.

He that means to underſtand what he *Sings* or *Plays*, muſt ſtudy to be perfect in the Knowledge of the *Scale* or *Gam-ut*, to have it perfect in his Memory without Book both forward and backward, and to diſtinguiſh the *Cliffs* and *Notes* as they ſtand in *Rule* or *Space*; for knowing the *Notes* Places, their Names are eaſily known.

The three Columns to the right hand of the *Scale* or *Gam-ut* are thus deſcribed:

The firſt Column is called *B duralis*, or *B ſharp*, as having no *Flat* in *B mi*, and has in it the Names of the Notes as they are called on the *Rules* and in the *Spaces*, aſcending and deſcending.

The ſecond Column is called *B naturalis*, or *B proper*, having a *B flat* in *B mi* only, which is put at the beginning of the Line with the *Cliff*; and in this Column likewiſe you have the *Names* of the Notes as they ſtand on *Rule* or in *Space*.

The third and laſt Column is called *B mollaris*, or *B fa*, having two *B flats*, the one in *B mi*, the other in *E la mi*, placed at the beginning with the *Cliff*; and here alſo you have the *Names* of the Notes.

In theſe three Columns, the *Names* of the Notes are changed according to the proper *Keys*. Alſo abſerve this for a General Rule, *That what Name any Note hath, the ſame Name properly hath its Eighth, either above or below it, be it in* Treble, Mean, Tenor, *or* Baſs.

THE

THE GAM-VT, OR SCALE OF MUSICK.

	Keys	Syllables	Cliffe	1	2	3
The Treble or highest Keyes.	aa	la mi re		la	la	mi
	gg	Sol re vt		Sol	Sol	la
	ff	fa vt		fa	fa	Sol
	E	la		la	mi	b fa
	D	la Sol		Sol	la	la
	C	Sol fa		fa	Sol	Sol
	B	fa ♯ mi		mi	b fa	b fa
	A	la mi re		la	la	mi
	G	Sol re vt	Cliffe	Sol	Sol	la
The Meane or middle Keyes.	F	fa vt		fa	fa	Sol
	E	la mi		la	mi	b fa
	D	la Sol re		Sol	la	la
	C	Sol fa vt	Cliffe	fa	Sol	Sol
	B	fa ♯ mi		mi	b fa	b fa
	A	la mi re		la	la	mi
	G	Sol re vt		Sol	Sol	la
The Basse or lowest Keyes.	F	fa vt	Cliffe	fa	fa	Sol
	E	la mi		la	mi	b fa
	D	Sol re		Sol	la	la
	C	fa vt		fa	Sol	Sol
	B	mi		mi	b fa	b fa
	A	re		la	la	mi
	Γ	Γam vt		Sol	Sol	la
	FF	fa vt		fa	fa	Sol
	EE	la mi		la	mi	fa
	DD	Sol re		Sol	la	la
	CC	fa vt		fa	Sol	Sol
				B Duralis, 1	B Naturalis, 2	B Mollaris, 3

A Second Table of the *Scale of MUSICK* called the *GAM-UT*, in which every *Key* or *Note* is put in its proper place upon the Five Lines on *Rule* and in *Space*, according to the two usual signed *Cleaves* or *Cliffs*, *viz.* the *Bassus* and the *Treble*, ascending from the lowest Note of the *Bass*, to the highest in the *Treble*.

D la sol, E la, F fa ut, G sol re ut, A la mi re.
F fa ut, G sol re ut, A la mi re, B fa b mi, C sol fa,
A la mi re, B fa b mi, C sol fa ut.
Treble.
D la sol re, E la mi,
B mi, C fa ut, D sol re, E la mi, F fa ut, G sol re ut,
Bassus.
CC fa ut, DD sol re, EE la mi, FF fa ut, Gam-ut, A re,

CHAP.

CHAP. II.

Of the Cliffs *or* Cleaves.

IN the *Gam-ut* (as I ſaid before) is contained three Septenaries of Letters, which are *G, A, B, C, D, E, F:* Theſe ſeven Letters are ſet at the beginning of each *Rule* and *Space*, and are called *Cliffs*; of theſe ſeven, four are only uſed, one of which is commonly plac'd at the beginning of every Line of any *Song* or *Leſſon*, either Vocal or Inſtrumental. The firſt is called *F fa ut* Cleave or Cliff, which is only proper to the *Baſs* or loweſt Part, and is thus marked 𝄢 on the fourth Line, at the beginning of *Songs* or *Leſſons*. The ſecond is the *C ſol fa ut*, which is proper to the Middle or Inner Parts, as *Tenor, Counter-Tenor*, or *Mean* and is thus ſigned or marked 𝄡 The third is the *G ſol re ut* Cleave or Cliff, which is only proper to the *Treble* or higheſt Part, and is ſigned or marked thus 𝄞 on the ſecond Line of the Song or Leſſon.

Theſe three *Cliffs* are called the *Three Signed Cliffs*, becauſe they are always ſet at the beginning of the Lines on which the *Song* or *Leſſon* is prick'd. *Cliff* or *Cleave* is derived from *Clavis* a Key, or Guide to underſtand the *Notes*.

From theſe *Cliffs*, the Places of all the Notes in your Song or Leſſon are underſtood, by proving your Notes from them, according to the Rule of the *Gam-ut*, either up or down.

A fourth *Cliff* is the *B Cliff*, which is proper to all Parts, as being of two Natures or Properties, that is to ſay, *flat* or *ſharp*, and doth only ſerve for the *flatting* and *ſharping* of Notes, and therefore it is called *B fa, B mi*; the *B fa* ſignifies *flat*, the *B mi*, *ſharp*. The *B fa*, or *B flat*, is known on *Rule* or *Space* by this mark [♭]; and the *B mi*, which is *ſharp*, by this [✳].

By theſe two *Rules*, you are to obſerve of them both; Firſt, the *B fa*, or *B flat*, doth alter both the Name and Property of the Notes before which it is placed, and is called *Fa*, making that Note half a Tone or Sound lower than it was before.

Secondly, the *B mi*, or *B ſharp*, alters the property of the Notes before which it is placed, but not the Name; for it is uſually placed either before *Fa* or *Sol*, and they retain their Names ſtill, but their Sound is raiſed half a Tone or Sound higher.

Note, That theſe two *B Cliffs* are placed not only at the beginning of the Lines with the other Cliffs, but are uſually put to ſeveral Notes in the middle of any Song or Leſſon for the *flatting* and *ſharping* them, as the Harmony of the *Muſick* requires.

CHAP. III.

A brief RULE for Proving the Notes in any Song, or Leſſon.

FIrſt, obſerve with which of the three uſual *Cliffs* your Song or Leſſon is ſigned with at the beginning; if it be with the *G ſol re ut* Cliff, then if the Note be above it, whoſe Name and Place you

you would know, you must begin at your Cliff, and assign to every Rule and Space a Note, according to the Rule of your *Gam-ut*, ascending till you come to that Rule or Space wherein the same Note is set: But if the Note be below your Cliff, then you must prove downwards to it, saying your *Gam-ut* backwards, assigning to each Rule and Space a Note, till you come to its place. So that by knowing in what place of your *Gam-ut* the Note is set, you will easily know its Name, the next Chapter directing you an *Infallible RULE* for it, and that by an easie and familiar Example.

CHAP. IV.

Containing a Plain and Easie RULE for the Naming your Notes in any Cliff.

HAving observed the foregoing Direction, of Proving your Notes to know their Places, you may easily know their Names also, if you will follow this RULE: First, observe that *Mi* is the *Principal* or *Master-Note*, which leads you to know all the rest; for having found out that, the other follow upon course; And this *Mi* hath its being in four several places, but it is but in one of them at a time, its proper place is in *B mi*; but if a *B fa*, which is a *B flat*, (as is mention'd in *Chap.* 2.) be put in that place, then it is removed into *E la mi*, which is its second place; but if a *B flat* be placed there also, then it is in its third place, which is *A la mi re*; if a *B flat* come there also, then it is removed into

its

its fourth place, which is *D la sol re*; so that in which of these it is, the next Notes above it ascending are *Fa sol la*, *Fa sol la*, twice, and then you meet with your *Mi* again, for it is found but once in eight Notes: In like manner, the Notes next below it descending are *La sol fa*, *La sol fa*, and then you have your *Mi* again. For your better understanding of which, observe this old Metre, whose Rules are plain, true, and easie.

To attain the Skill *of Musick's Art,*
Learn Gam-ut *up and down by heart,*
Thereby to learn your Rules *and* Spaces,
Notes *Names are known, knowing their Places.*
No Man can Sing true at first sight,
Unless he Name his Notes *aright;*
Which soon is learnt, if that your Mi
You know its Place where e'er it be.

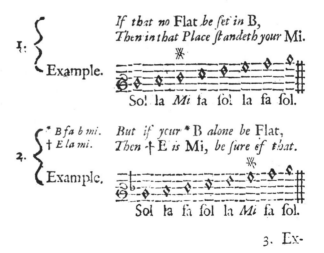

1. *If that no* Flat *be set in* B,
Then in that Place standeth your Mi.

Example.

Sol la *Mi* fa sol la fa sol.

2. *If your* * B *alone be* Flat,
Then † E *is* Mi, *be sure of that.*

* *B fa b mi.*
† *E la mi.*

Example.

Sol la fa sol la *Mi* fa sol.

3. Ex-

3. * *A la mi re.* *If both be* Flat, *your* B *and* E,
*Then** A *is* Mi, *here you may ſee.*

Example.

La *Mi* fa ſol la fa ſol la.

4. * *D la ſol.* *If all be* Flat, E, A, *and* B,
Then Mi *alone doth ſtand in* * D.

Example.

La fa ſol la *Mi* fa ſol la.

The firſt three Notes above your Mi
Are Fa ſol la, *here you may ſee;*
The next three under Mi *that fall,*
Them La ſol fa *you ought to call.*

Example.

Sol la *Mi* fa ſol la fa ſol fa la ſol fa *Mi* la ſol fa.

If you'l Sing True without all blame,
You call all Eighths *by the ſame Name.*

Exam-

Example of the Eighths.

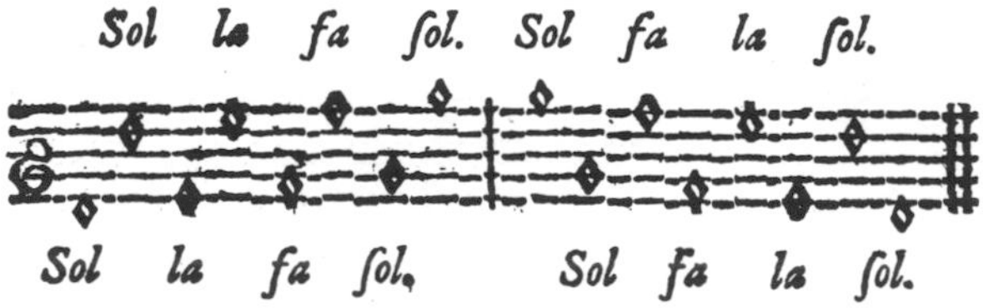
Sol la fa sol. Sol fa la sol.
Sol la fa sol. Sol fa la sol.

First learn by Cliffs *to Name your* Notes
By Rules *and* Spaces *right;*
Then Tune with TIME, *to Ground your* Skill
For Musick's *sweet Delight.*

These *Rules* and *Examples* being seriously perused by the Learner, will infallibly direct him in the right *naming* of his *Notes*, which is a very great help to the Singer; for nothing makes him sooner mistake his Tune in Singing, than the miss-naming his Notes: And therefore take this one *Rule* more for the naming your Notes, by finding your *Mi* in its several places in any Cliff whatsoever, be it *Bass*, *Treble*, or any *Inward Part*, there being no *Song* prick'd down for any Part that does not employ some of the Five Lines in the following Example. The several Parts are demonstrated by the little *Arches* or *Columns* on the right side of the Example.

Ano

Another Example for Naming the *NOTES* in any *Cliff.*

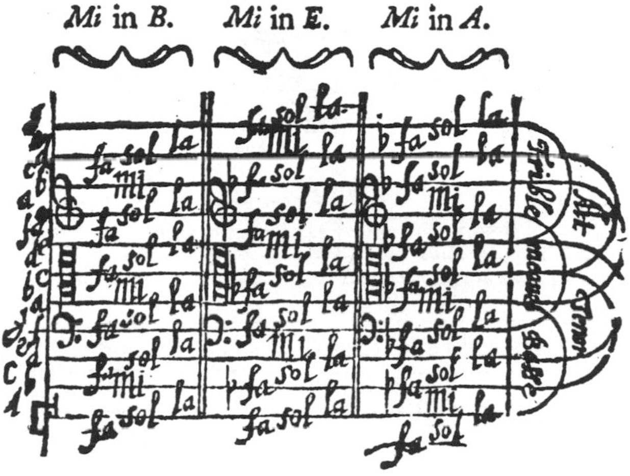
Mi in *B.*
Mi in *E.*
Mi in *A.*
Trible
Meane
Alt
Tenor
Baſſe

This *Example* expreſſes the Names of the *Notes* in the three Removes of *Mi.* I have ſeen *Songs* with four *Flats*, (as is before mentioned) *viz.* in *B mi*, *E la mi*, *A la mi re*, and *D la ſol re*; but this fourth place of *D la ſol re* is very ſeldom uſed, and ſuch *Songs* may be termed *Irregular* as to the naming the Notes, (being rather intended for Inſtruments than Voices) and therefore not fit to be propoſed to young *Beginners* to Sing. And becauſe I will omit nothing that may be uſeful to *Practitioners*, I have ſet down a third Example of Naming the *Notes* in all Parts, as the Flats are aſſigned to the *Cliffs*.

An

An exact TABLE of the *Names* of the *Notes* in all the uſual *Cliffs*, expreſſed in the Six ſeveral Parts of Muſick.

Treble. G ſol re ut *Cliff on the ſecond Line.*

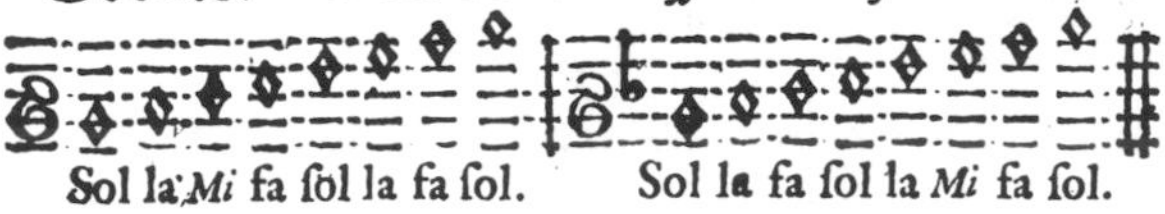
Sol la *Mi* fa ſol la fa ſol.
Sol la fa ſol la *Mi* fa ſol.

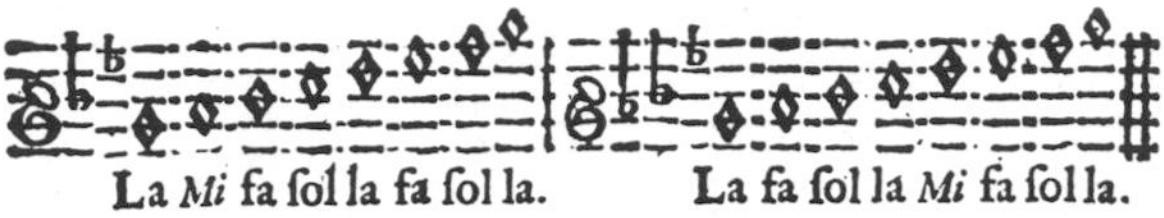
La *Mi* fa ſol la fa ſol la.
La fa ſol la *Mi* fa ſol la.

Altus. C ſol fa ut *Cliff on the firſt Line.*

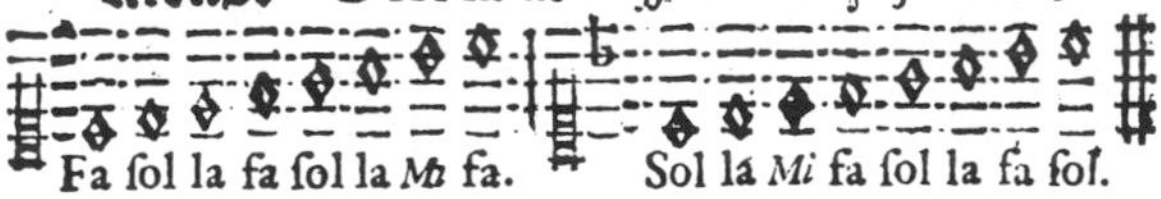
Fa ſol la fa ſol la *Mi* fa.
Sol la *Mi* fa ſol la fa ſol.

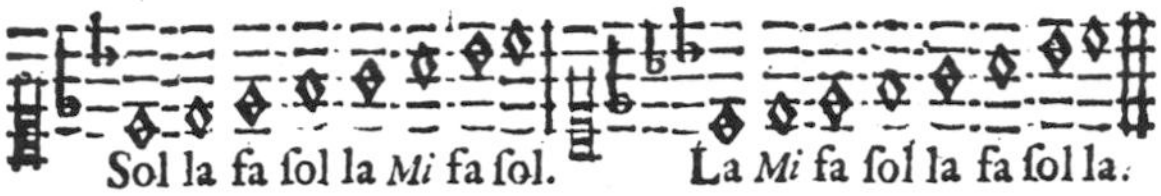
Sol la fa ſol la *Mi* fa ſol.
La *Mi* fa ſol la fa ſol la.

Mean. C ſol fa ut *Cliff on the ſecond Line.*

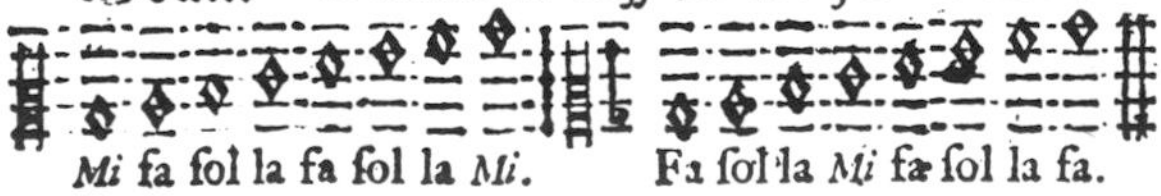
Mi fa ſol la fa ſol la *Mi*.
Fa ſol la *Mi* fa ſol la fa.

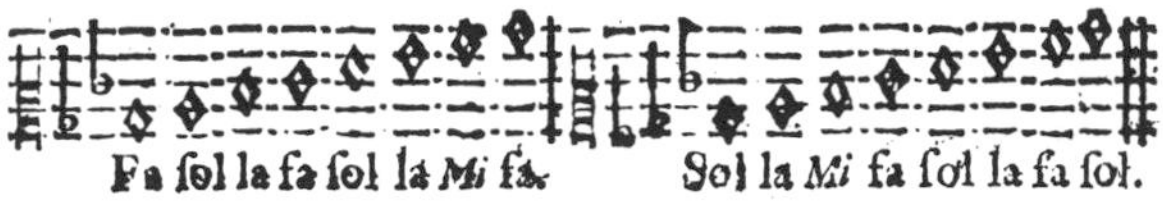
Fa ſol la fa ſol la *Mi* fa.
Sol la *Mi* fa ſol la fa ſol.

Counter-

Counter-Tenor. C sol fa ut *Cliff on the 3d Line.*

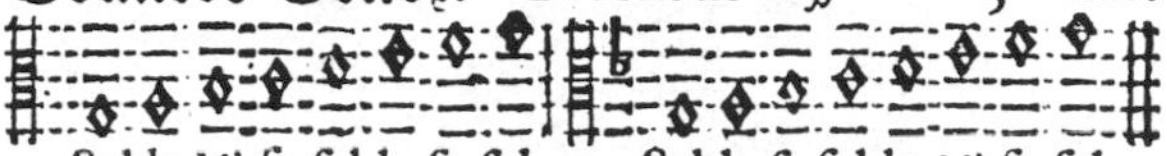
Sol la *Mi* fa sol la fa sol.
Sol la fa sol la *Mi* fa sol.

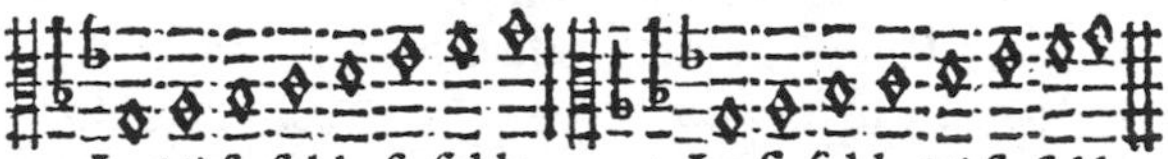
La *Mi* fa sol la fa sol la.
La fa sol la *Mi* fa sol la.

Tenor. C sol fa ut *Cliff on the fourth Line.*

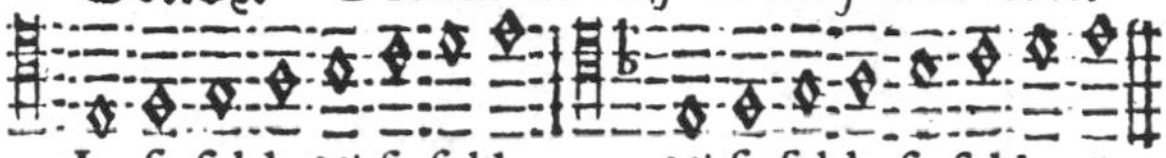
La fa sol la *Mi* fa sol la.
Mi fa sol la fa sol la *Mi*.

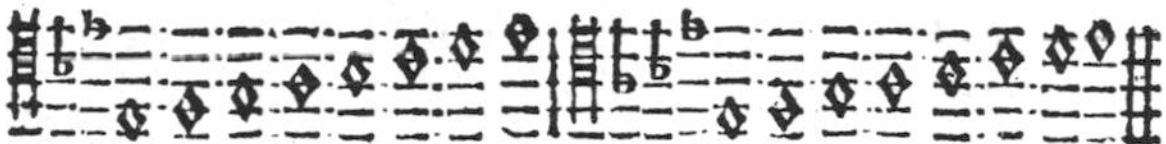
Fa sol la *Mi* fa sol la fa.
Fa sol la fa sol la *Mi* fa.

Bass. F fa ut *Cliff on the fourth Line.*

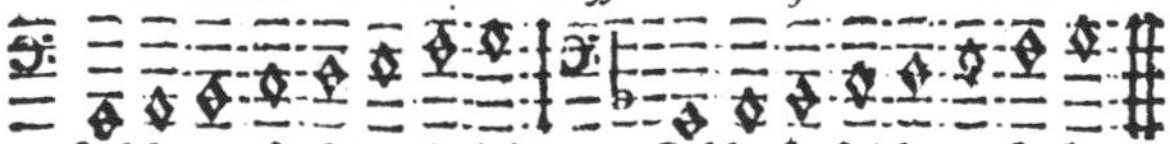
Sol la *Mi* fa sol la fa sol.
Sol la fa sol la *Mi* fa sol.

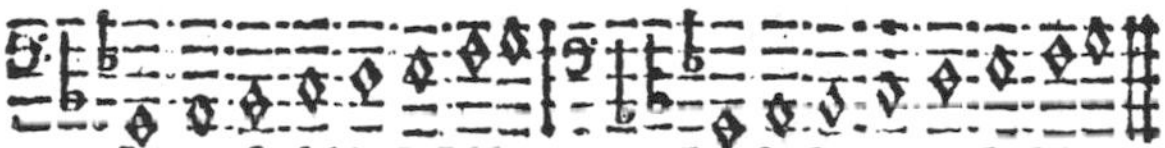
La *Mi* fa sol la fa sol la.
La fa sol la *Mi* fa sol la.

CHAP.

CHAP. V.

Of Tuning the Voice.

THus having briefly given you plain and familiar Rules for the underſtanding the nature and uſe of the *Gam-ut*, it will be neceſſary, before I ſet down your firſt plain *Songs*, to inſert a word or two concerning the *Tuning of the Voice*, in regard none can attain the right guiding or ordering his *Voice*, in the *riſing* and *falling* of ſeveral *Sounds* which are in *Muſick*, at firſt, without the help of another *Voice*, or *Inſtrument*. They are both of them extraordinary helps: But the *Voice* of a skilful *Artiſt* is firſt to be preferr'd; yet the *Voice* guided by the *ſound* of an *Inſtrument*, may do well, if the Learner have Skill thereon himſelf to expreſs the ſeveral *ſounds*, ſo that his Ear and Voice go along with the *Inſtrument*, in the *aſcending* and *deſcending* of the ſeveral *Notes* or *Sounds*. And (if not) if an *Inſtrument* be ſounded by another who is an *Artiſt*, ſo the Learner hath a good *Ear* to guide his *Voice* in *unity* to the *ſound* of the *Inſtrument*, it will with a little Practice (by ſometimes ſinging with, and ſometimes without,) guide his *Voice* into a perfect *Harmony*, to ſing plain *Song* with exactneſs; I mean by Tuning his Notes perfectly, Aſcending and Deſcending, and in raiſing or falling of a *Third*, a *Fourth*, a *Fifth*, or a *Sixth*, *&c.* as in the following *Plain Songs* they are ſet down. At the firſt guiding the Voice therein, it will much help you if you obſerve this *Rule*: For a *Third* aſcending, which

which is from *Sol* to *Mi*, at your first Tuning sound by degrees all three Notes, as *Sol La Mi*, then at second Tuning leave out *La* the middle Note, and so you will Tune from *Sol* to *Mi*, which is a *Third*. This Rule serves for the rising of *Fourths* or *Fifths*, *&c.* as your third Plain Song in the next Page directs.

Observe, that in the Tuning your Voice you strive to have it clear.

Also in the expressing your Voice, or tuning of Notes, let the Sound come clear from your throat, and not through the teeth, by sucking in your breath, for that is a great obstruction to the clear utterance of the Voice.

Lastly, observe that in tuning your first Note of your Plain Song, you equal it so to the pitch of your Voice, that when you come to your highest Note, you may reach it without squeaking, and your lowest Note without grumbling.

The Three usual Plain SONGS *for Tuning the* VOICE, *with the proper* Letters *of the Names of the* Notes.

First.

S L M F S L F S S F L S F M L S L S

Second.

S M L F M S F L L F S M F L M S L S

Third ascending. 3
4
5
S L M S M S L M F S F S L M F S S S
6.
7
S L M F S L S L S L M F S L F S F
8
Descending.
S L M F S L. F S S S S F L S L S F L S S S
S F L S F S F S F L S F M S M
8
S F L S F M L S L S F L S F M L S S S
7 6 5 4 3 2
F S L S S S F S M S L S.

CHAP. VI.

Of Tones, or Tunes of Notes.

OBserve, that the two *B Cliffs* before-mention'd are used in *Songs* for the *flatting* and *sharping* Notes. The property of the *B flat* is to change *Mi* into *Fa*, making that Note to which it is joyned a *Semi-*

Semitone or half a Note lower; and the *B sharp* raiseth the Note before which it is set a *Semitone* or half a *sound higher*, but alters not its Name; so that from *Mi* to *Fa*, and likewise from *La* to *Fa*, is but a *Semitone* or a half Note; between any two other Notes it is a perfect *Tone* or *Sound*, as from *Fa* to *Sol*, from *Sol* to *La*, from *La* to *Mi*, are whole *Tones*, which is a perfect *sound*. And this may be easily distinguished; if you try it on the Frets of a *Viol* or *Lute*, you shall perceive plainly that there goes two *Frets* to the stopping of a whole *Note*, and but one *Fret* to a half *Note*; so that it is observed, that *Mi* and *Fa* serve only for the *flatting* or *sharping* all Notes in the *Scale*, and they being rightly understood, the other *Notes* are easily applied to them; for if *G sol re ut* have a sharp set before it, it's the same in sound with *A la mi re* flat; and *B fa b mi* flat is the same with *A la mi re* sharp, and *C fa ut* sharp is *D sol re* flat, *&c.* as being of one and the same sound, or stopped upon one and the same Fret of the *Viol* or *Violin*.

Unisons. For Example. *Octaves.*

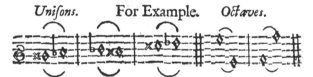

For Discourse of the Cords *and* Discords, *I shall only name them in this part of my Book.*

PErfect *Cords* are these; a *Fifth*, an *Eighth*, with their *Compounds* or *Octaves*.

Imperfect *Cords* are these; a *Third*, a *Sixth*, with their *Compounds*: All other Distances reckon'd from the *Bass* are *Discords*.

A *Diapason* is a perfect *Eighth*, containing five whole *Tones*, and two half *Tones*, that are in all seven natural *Sounds* or *Notes* besides the Ground, what *flats* or *sharps* soe'er there be.

For a further Discourse, I refer you to Mr. *Simpson's Compendium*, or *The Art of Descant*; my purpose here being only to set down the Rules for the *Theorick Part* of *Musick*, so far as is necessary to be understood by young Practitioners in *Vocal* or *Instrumental Musick*. I shall in the next Chapter give an account of the *Notes*, their *Time* and *Proportions*.

CHAP. VII.

The Notes; their Names, Number, Measure, and Proportions.

Semibreve.
Minim.
Crotchet.
Quaver.
Semiquaver.
&c.

Measure, in this Science, is a Quantity of the length or shortness of *Time*, either by Natural Sounds, pronounced by the Voice; or Artificial, upon Instruments; which *Measure* is by a certain Motion of the hand or foot expressed in variety of Notes. These Notes in *Musick* have two Names, one for *Tune*, the other for *Time*, *Measure* or *Proportion* of Notes to certain Sounds. The Names of *Notes* in Tuning I have set down in the former Chapter, being four, *Sol*, *La*, *Mi*, *Fa*: Those

Those in the Measure or Proportion of Time are Six, as a *Semibreve*, *Minim*, *Crotchet*, *Quaver*, *Semiquaver*, and *Demisemiquaver*, as they are expressed upon five Lines at the beginning of this Chapter.

There were three other *Notes* formerly in use, as a *Large*, a *Long*, and a *Breve*, which that you may not be ignorant of them, I will let you know their Value and Proportion of *Time*. A *Large* contains two *Longs*, a *Long* two *Breves*, and a *Breve* two *Semibreves*, so that a *Large* contains 8 *Semibreves*, which is a Sound too long to be held by any Voice or Instrument except the *Organ*, the *Semibreve* being the longest Note now in use; and called the *Master-Note*, or a *Whole Time*: I shall give you an account what Proportion it bears in *Time*, as likewise what each *Note* bears in Proportion over each other, which you must be well acquainted with before you can beat *Time* right, which I shall speak of in *Chap.* 9. But observe this following Example. As,

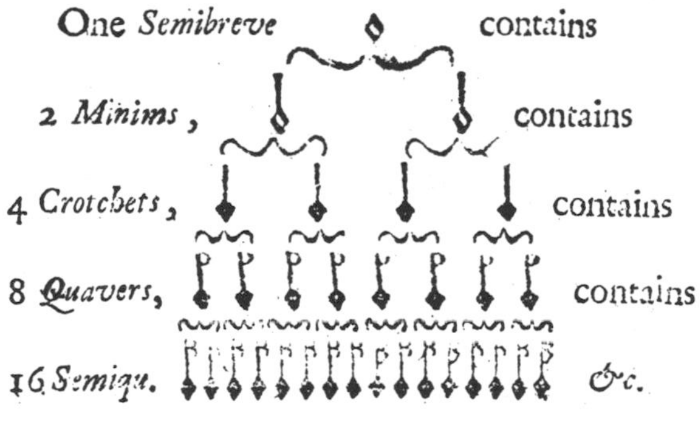
One *Semibreve* contains
2 *Minims*, contains
4 *Crotchets*, contains
8 *Quavers*, contains
16 *Semiqu.* &c.

CHAP. VIII.

Of the Rests *or* Pauses, *of* Pricks *or* Points *of* Addition, *and Notes of* Syncopation.

PAuses or *Rests* are silent *Characters*, or an *artificial* omission of the *Voice* or *Sound*, proportion'd to the *Measure* of other *Notes* according to their several Distinctions; which that the Performer may not Rest or Pause too long or short before he Plays or Sings again, there is a *Rest* assigned to every *Note:* As the *Semibreve Rest*, which is expressed by a Stroak drawn downwards from any one of the Five Lines half through the Space between Line and Line; the *Minim Rest* is ascending upward from the Line; the *Crotchet Rest* is turned off like a Tenter-hook to the right hand, and the *Quaver Rest* to the left; the *Semiquaver Rest* with a double Stroak to the left; and the *Demisemiquaver Rest* with a triple Stroak to the left. Now whenever you come to any of these *Rests*, you must cease Playing or Singing till you have counted them silently according to their value in *Time* before you play again; as when you meet with a *Semibreve Rest*, you must be as long silent as you would be performing the *Semibreve*, before you Sing or Play again; so of a *Crotchet*, a *Quaver*, or the like. If the Stroak be drawn from one Line to another, then 'tis two *Semibreves*; if from one Line to a third, then 'tis four *Semibreves:* As in this following Example.

8 *Semi-*

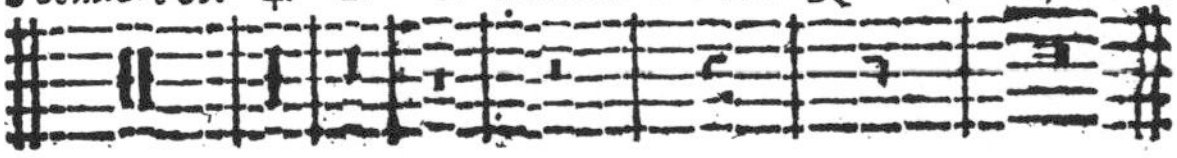
Semibreve. 4. 2. 1. Minim. Crotchet. Quaver. Semiquaver.

Now you must observe, That when you meet with a *Semibreve Rest* made in *Tripla Time*, or in any other sort of *Time* besides plain *Common Time*, it serves for a whole Bar of that *Time* which you Sing or Play in, altho' the *Time* may be longer or shorter than a *Semibreve*; or if 'tis drawn from Line to Line, (like two *Semibreve Rests*) it serves for two Bars, and no more nor less: so for four or eight Bars, or more, according as you find it mark'd down.

The *Prick* of *Perfection*, or *Point* of *Addition*, is a little *Point* placed always on the right side of the *Note*, and adds to the Value of the *Sound* half as much as it was before; for as one *Semibreve* contains two *Minims*, when this *Point* is added to it it must be held as long as three *Minims*; so of *Crotchets*, *Quavers*, &c. as in this Example.

Prick'd Semibreve. Minim. Crotchet. Quaver.
&c.

Sometimes you will meet with a *Prick* or *Point* placed at the beginning of a Bar, which belongs to the last Note in the preceding Bar.

As for Example.

The same by NOTES.

Notes of *Syncopation*, or *Driving-Notes*, are, when your Hand or Foot is taken up, or put down, while the *Note* is sounding, which is very awkward to a Young Practitioner; but when once he can do this well, he may think himself pretty Perfect in keeping *Time*. For an Example, take this following Lesson.

Of the Tying of Notes.

The same Notes unty'd.

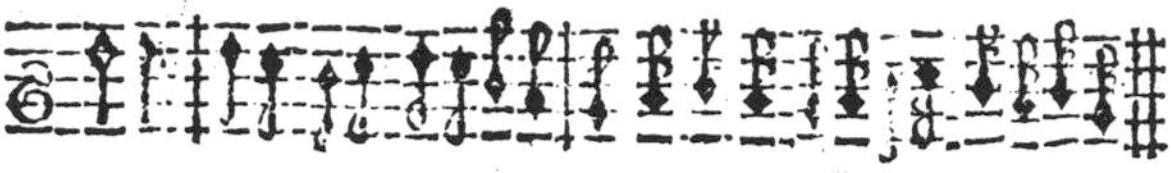

This

This Example ſhews, that many times in Songs or Leſſons, two, four, or more *Quavers* or *Semiquavers* are tied together by a long ſtroak drawn through their Tails; and tho' they be ſo, they are the ſame with the other, and are ſo tied for the benefit of the Sight when many *Quavers* or *Semiquavers* happen together, not altering the Meaſure or Proportion of *Time.*

CHAP. IX.

Of the MOODS, *or* Proportions *of the* Time *or* Meaſure *of* NOTES.

THis part of Muſick, called *Time*, is ſo neceſſary to be underſtood, that unleſs the Practitioner arrive to a Perfection in it, he will never be able to Play with any delight to himſelf, or at leaſt to a Skilful Ear; the Uſe of it rendring *Muſick* ſo infinitely more Pleaſing and Delightful, which to obtain, I have ſet down theſe following *Inſtructions.*

That there is but two *Moods* or *Characters* by which *Time* is diſtinguiſhed, *viz. Common-Time*, and *Tripla-Time*, all other Variations and Diſtinctions of *Time* (like ſo many Rivulets) take their Original from theſe two; the Marks of which are always placed at the beginning of your *Song* or *Leſſon.*

Firſt, I ſhall ſpeak of *Common-Time*, which may be reckon'd three ſeveral ſorts; the firſt and ſloweſt of all is marked thus C: 'Tis meaſured by by a *Semibreve*, which you must divide into four equal Parts, telling *one*, *two*, *three*, *four*, distinctly, putting your Hand or Foot down when you tell *one*, and taking it up when you tell *three*, so that you are as long down as up. Stand by a large Chamber-Clock, and beat your Hand or Foot (as I have before observed) to the slow Motions of the Pendulum, telling *one*, *two*, with your Hand down as you hear it strike, and *three*, *four*, with your Hand up; which Measure I would have you observe in this *slow* sort of *Common-Time*: Also you must observe to have your Hand or Foot down at the beginning of every Bar.

The second sort of *Common-Time* is a little faster, which is known by the *Mood*, having a stroak drawn through it, thus ₵.

The third sort of *Common-Time* is quickest of all, and then the *Mood* is retorted thus Ↄꟾ; you may tell *one*, *two*, *three*, *four*, in a Bar, almost as fast as the regular Motions of a Watch. The *French Mark* for this retorted *Time*, is a large Figure of 2.

There are two other sorts of *Time* which may be reckoned amongst *Common-Time* for the equal division of the Bar with the Hand or Foot up and down: The first of which is called *Six to four*, each Bar containing six *Crotchets*, or six *Quavers*, three to be sung with the Hand down, and three up, and is marked thus $\frac{6}{4}$, but very brisk, and is always used in *Jigs*.

The other sort is called *Twelve to eight*, each Bar containing twelve *Quavers*, six with the Hand down, and six up, and marked thus $^{12}_{8}$.

These are all the *Moods* of *Common-Time* now in use. The length of your *Notes* you must perfectly get before you can keep *Time* right; for the which, I refer you to *Chap.* 7.

Tripla-Time, that you may understand it right, I will distinguish into two sorts: The first and slowest of which is measured by three *Minims* in each Bar, or such a quantity of lesser *Notes* as amount to the value of three *Minims*, or one *Pointed Semibreve*, telling *one*, *two*, with your Hand down, and up with it at the *third*; so that you are as long again with your Hand or Foot down as up. This sort of *Time* is marked thus $^{3}_{2}$.

The second sort is faster, and the *Minims* become *Crotchets*, so that a Bar contains three *Crotchets*, or one *Pointed Minim*; 'tis marked thus 3, or thus 31. Sometimes you will meet with three *Quavers* in a Bar, which is marked as the *Crotchets*, only Sung as fast again.

There is another sort of *Time* which is used in *Instrumental Musick*, call *Nine to six*, marked thus $^{9}_{6}$, each Bar containing nine *Quavers* or *Crotchets*, six to be Play'd with the Foot down, and three up: This I also reckon amongst *Tripla-Time*, because there is as many more down as up.

These, I think, are all the *Moods* now in use, both *Common* and *Tripla-Time:* But 'tis necessary for the Young Practitioner to observe, That in the

the middle of ſome *Songs* or *Tunes* he will meet with *Quavers* joyn'd together three by three, with a Figure of 3 marked over every three *Quavers*, or (it may be) only over the firſt three: Theſe muſt be performed, each three *Quavers* to the value of one *Crotchet*, which in *Common-Time* is the ſame with *Twelve to eight*, and in *Tripla-Time* the ſame with *Nine to ſix*.

A Perfection in theſe ſeveral *Moods* cannot be obtained without a diligent Practice, which may be done at any time when you do not Sing or Play, only telling *one*, *two*, *three*, *four*, or *one*, *two*, *three*, and Beating to it; (as I have before obſerved.) Alſo the Young Practitioner muſt take care to Sing or Play with one that is perfect in it, and ſhun thoſe which are not better than himſelf.

CHAP. X.

Of the ſeveral Adjuncts *and* Characters *uſed in* MUSICK.

1 A *Direct* is uſually put at the end of the Line, and ſerves to direct to the place of the firſt Note on the next Line, and are thus made:

2. *Bars* are of two ſorts, *ſingle* and *double*. The *ſingle Bars* ſerve to divide the *Time* according to the Mea-

Meaſure of the *Semibreve*. The *double Bars* are ſet to divide the ſeveral *Strains* or *Stanza's* of the *Songs* and *Leſſons*; and are thus made :

3. A *Repeat* is thus marked 𝄋, and is uſed to ſignifie, that ſuch a part of a Song or Leſſon muſt be played or ſung over again from the Note over which it is placed.

4. A *Tye* is of two Uſes; Firſt, when the Note is driven, or the Time ſtruck in the middle of the Note; it is uſual to tye two *Minims*, or a *Minim* and a *Crotchet* together; as thus:

The ſecond ſort of *Tyes*, is when two or more Notes are to be ſung to one Syllable, or two Notes or more to be play'd with once drawing the Bow on the *Viol* or *Violin*, as thus:

Thou art not Kind, but Cruel.

5. A *Hold* is thus made 𝄐, and is placed over the Note which the *Author* intends ſhould be held to a longer Meaſure than the Note contains; and over the laſt Note of a Leſſon.

6. The

6. The *Figures* uſually placed over *Notes* in the *Thorow-Baſs* of *Songs* or *Ayres* for the *Organ* or *Theorbo*, is to direct the *Performer* to ſtrike in other Parts to thoſe Notes, as *Thirds*, *Sixths*, *&c.* with *Sharps* and *Flats*; as thus:

♯3 65 78 43 4♯3

I ſhall here conclude the Firſt Part, *wherein I have ſet down what is needful to be underſtood of the Theorick Part of* Muſick *in the plaineſt and eaſieſt Method that I could; not doubting but by it, and a little Aſſiſtance of ſome already Skill'd in* Muſick, *to Guide you to the Practick.*

A brief Discourse of the Italian *manner of Singing; wherein is set down the Use of those Graces in Singing, as the* Trill *and* Gruppo *used in* Italy, *and now in* England: *Written some Years since by an* English *Gentleman who had lived long in* Italy, *and being returned, Taught the same here.*

The Proem *to the said Discourse is to this effect.*

HItherto I have not put forth to the view of the World those Fruits of my Musick Studies, employ'd about that Noble manner of Singing which I learnt of my Master the famous *Scipione del Palla* in *Italy*; nor my Compositions of *Ayres* Composed by me, which I saw frequently practised by the most famous Singers in *Italy*, both Men and Women: But seeing many of them go about maim'd and spoil'd, and that those long-winding Points were ill performed, I therefore devised to avoid that old manner of running *Division* which has been hitherto used, being indeed more proper for Wind and Stringed Instruments, than for the Voice: And seeing that there is made now adays an indifferent and confus'd use of those excellent *Graces* and *Ornaments* to the good and true manner of *Singing*, which we call *Trills* and *Grupps*, *Exclamations* of *Increasing* and

and *Abating* of the Voice, of which I do intend in this my Discourse to leave some Foot-prints, that others may attain to this excellent manner of Singing: To which manner I have framed my last *Ayres* for one Voice to the *Theorbo*, not following that old way of *Composition*, whose Musick not suffering the Words to be understood by the Hearers, for the multitude of Divisions made upon short and long Syllables, though by the Vulgar such Singers were cryed up for Famous. But I have endeavour'd in those my late Compositions to bring in a kind of Musick, by which Men might, as it were, Talk in Harmony, using in that kind of Singing a certain noble neglect of the Song, (as I have often heard at *Florence* by the Actors in their Singing *Opera's*) in which I endeavour'd the Imitation of the Conceit of the Words, seeking out the Cords more or less Passionate, according to the meaning of them, having concealed in them so much as I could the *Art of Descant*, and paused or stayed the Consonances or Cords upon long Syllables, avoiding the short, and observing the same Rule in making the passages of Division by some few *Quavers* to Notes and to Cadences, not exceeding the value of a quarter or half a *Semibreve* at most. / But, as I said before, those long windings and turnings of the Voice are ill used; for I have observed, that Divisions have been Invented, not because they are necessary unto a good fashion of Singing, but rather for a certain tickling of the Ears of those who do not well understand what it is to sing Passionately; for if they did, undoubtedly Divisions would have been abhorr'd, there being

nothing

nothing more contrary to Paſſion than they are, yet in ſome kind of Muſick leſs Paſſionate or Affectuous; and upon long Syllables, not ſhort, and in final Cadences ſome ſhort Points of Diviſion may be uſed, not at all adventures, but upon the Practice of the Deſcant; but to think of them firſt in thoſe things that a man will ſing by himſelf, and to faſhion out the manner of them, and not to promiſe a man's ſelf that this Deſcant will bear it: For to the good manner of Compoſing and Singing in this way, the underſtanding of this Conceit, and the humour of the Words, as well in paſſionate Cords, as paſſionate Expreſſions in Singing, doth more avail than Deſcant; I have made uſe of it only to accord 2 Parts together, & to avoid certain notable Errors, and bind certain Diſcords for the accompanying of the Paſſion, more than to uſe the Art: And certain it is, that an *Ayre* Compoſed in this manner upon the Conceit of the Words, by one that hath a good faſhion of Singing, will work a better effect and delight more than another made with all the Art of Deſcant, where the Humour or Conceit of the Words is not minded.

The original of which Defect (if I deceive not my ſelf) is hence occaſioned, becauſe the Muſician doth not well poſſeſs and make himſelf Maſter of that which he is to Sing; for if he did ſo, undoubtedly he would not run into ſuch Errors as moſt eaſily he falleth into, who hath framed to himſelf a manner of Singing: For Example, altogether Paſſionate, with a General Rule, that in Encreaſing and Abating the Voice, and in Exclamations, is the foundation of Paſſion, doth always uſe them in every ſort of Muſick, not diſcerning whether the words require it: Whereas thoſe that well underſtand the conceit and meaning of the words, know our Defects, and can diſtinguiſh where the Paſſion is more or leſs required. Which ſort of People we ſhould endeavour to pleaſe with all diligence, and more to eſteem their Praiſe, than the Applauſe of the ignorant Vulgar.

Thus *Art* admitteth no Mediocrity; and how much the more Curioſities are in it, by reaſon of the Excellence thereof, with ſo much the more labour and love ought we, the Profeſſors thereof, to find them out: Which love hath moved me (conſidering that from Writings we receive the light of all *Science*, and of all *Art*) to leave behind me this little light in the enſuing Notes and Diſcourſes; it being my intention to ſhew ſo much as appertaineth to him who maketh the profeſſion of Singing alone, to the Harmony of the *Theorbo*, or other Stringed Inſtrument, ſo that he be already entred into the Theory of *Muſick*, and Play ſufficiently. Not that this cannot alſo be attained by long Practiſe, as it is ſeen that many, both Men and Women, have done, and yet this they attain is but unto a certain degree; but becauſe the Theory of the Writings conduceth unto the attaining of that degree; and becauſe in the Profeſſion of a *Singer*, (in regard of the Excellence thereof) not only particular Things are of uſe, but they all together do better it: Therefore to proceed in order, thus will I ſay;

That

That the chiefest Foundations, and most important Grounds of this Art, are the *Tuning* of the *Voice* in all the *Notes*; not only that it be neither too high nor too low, but that there be a good manner of *Tuning* it used. Which *Tuning* being used for the most part in two fashions, we will consider both of the one and the other; and by the following Notes, will shew that which to me seemeth more proper to other Effects.

There are some therefore, that in the *Tuning* of the first *Note*, tune it a *Third* under: Others tune the said first *Note* in his proper Tune, always increasing it in Loudness, saying, That this is the good way of putting forth the *Voice* gracefully.

Concerning the first: Since it is not a General Rule, because it agrees not in many Cords, altho' in such places as it may be used, it is now become so ordinary, that in stead of being a Grace (because some stay too long in the third *Note* under, whereas it should be but lightly touched,) it is rather tedious to the Ear; and that for Beginners in particular, it ought seldom to be used: But in stead of it, as being more strange, I would chuse the second for the increasing of the Voice.

Now because I have not contain'd my self within ordinary terms, and such as others have used, yea rather have continually searched after Novelty, so much as was possible for me, so that the Novelty may fitly serve to the better obtaining of the *Musicians* end, that is, to delight and move the Affections of the Mind, I have found it to be a more affectuous way to tune the *Voice* by a contrary effect to the other, that is, to tune the first Note in its proper

Tune, diminiſhing it, becauſe *Exclamation* is the principal means to move the *Affection*; and *Exclamation* properly is no other thing but the ſlacking of the Voice, to reinforce it ſomewhat more. Whereas increaſing of the Voice in the *Treble* Part, eſpecially in feigned Voices, doth oftentimes become harſh and unſufferable to the Hearing, as upon divers occaſions I have heard. Undoubtedly therefore, as an Affection more proper to move, it will work a better effect to tune the Voice, diminiſhing it, rather than increaſing of it: Becauſe in the firſt of theſe ways now mentioned, when a man increaſes the Voice to make an Exclamation, it is needful that in Slacking of it he increaſe it the more; and therefore I have ſaid, that it ſheweth harſh and rough. But in the diminiſhing of the Voice it will work a quite contrary effect, becauſe when the Voice is ſlacked, then to give it a little ſpirit, will always make it more paſſionate. Beſides that alſo, uſing ſometimes one, ſometimes another, variety may be uſed, which is very neceſſary in this *Art*, ſo that it be directed to the ſaid End.

So then, if this be the greateſt part of that Grace in Singing, which is apt to move the Affection of the Mind, in thoſe conceits certainly where there is moſt uſe of ſuch Affections or Paſſions, and if it be demonſtrated with ſuch lively Reaſons, a new Conſequence is hence inferred, That from Writings of men likewiſe may be learnt that moſt neceſſary Grace, which cannot be diſcrib'd in better manner, and more clearly for the underſtanding thereof; and yet it may be perfectly attain'd unto: So that after the Study of the Theory, and after theſe Rules,

Rules, they may be put in Practice, by which a man grows more perfect in all Arts, especially in the Profession of a perfect Singer, be it Man or Woman.

More Languid. A livelier Exclamation. *For Example.*

Cor m-io deh non langui——re, gui——re.

Of Tuning therefore with more or less Grace, and how it may be done in the aforesaid manner, Tryal may be made in the above-written Notes with the words under them, *Cor mio, deh non languire.* For in the first *Minim* with the *Prick* you may tune *Cor mio*, diminishing it by little and little, and in the falling of the *Crotchet* increase the Voice with a little more spirit, and it will become an *Exclamation* passionate enough, tho' in a Note that falls but one degree: But much more sprightful will it appear in the word *deh*, by holding of a Note that falls not by one degree; as likewise 'twill become most sweet by the taking of the greater *Sixth* that falls by a leap. Which thing I have observed, not only to shew to others what a thing *Exclamation* is, and from whence it grows; but also that there may be two kinds of it, one more passionate than the other; as well by the manner in which they are described, or tuned in the one way or other; as also by imitation of the word, when it shall have a signification suitable to the Conceit. Besides that, *Exclamations* may be used in all Passionate Musick, by one General Rule in all *Minims* and *Crotchets* with a *Prick* falling; and they shall be far more Passionate by the following Note which runneth, than they can be in *Semibreves*; in which 'twill be fitter for increasing and diminishing the Voice, without using the *Exclamations*. Yet by consequence understand, that in *Airy* Musick, or *Corants* to dance, in stead of these Passions, there is to be used only a lively chearful kind of Singing, which is carried and ruled by the *Air* it self. In the which, though sometimes there may be place for some *Exclamation*, that liveliness of Singing is in that place to be omitted, and not any Passion to be used which savoureth of *Languishment*. Whereupon we see how necessary a certain Judgment is for a Musician, which sometimes useth to prevail above Art. As also we may perceive by the foregoing Notes, how much greater Grace the four first *Quavers* have upon the second Syllable of the word *Languire*, (being so stayed by the second *Quaver* with a *Prick*) than the four last equal *Quavers* so Printed for Example. But because there are many things which are used in a good fashion of Singing, which, because there is found in them a greater Grace, being describ'd in some one manner, make a contrary effect one to the other; whereupon we use to say of a Man, That he Sings with much Grace, or little Grace: These things will occasion me at this time, first to demonstrate in what fashion I have described the *Trill* and the *Grup*; and the

man-

manner used by me to teach them to those who have been interessed in my House; and further, all other the more necessary Effects: So that I leave not unexpressed any Curiosity which I have observed.

Trill, or Plain Shake. *Gruppo, or Double Relish.*

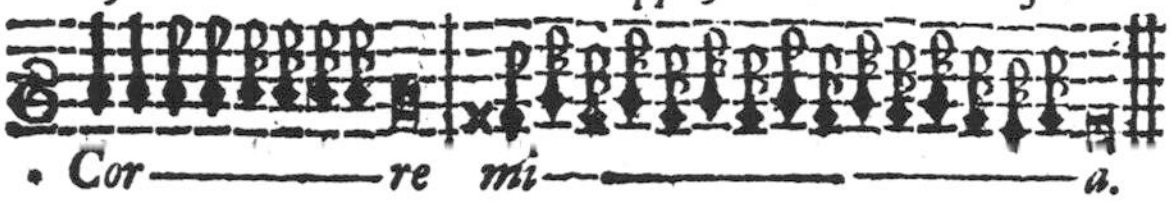
Cor——re mi——a.

The *Trill* describ'd by me is upon one *Note* only; that is to say, to begin with the first *Crotchet*, and to beat every *Note* with the *throat* upon the Vowel [*a*] unto the last *Breve*; as likewise the *Gruppo*, or *Double Relish*. *Which* Trill *and* Gruppo *was exactly learned, and exquisitely performed by my Scholars.* So that if it be true, that *Experience is the Teacher of all Things*, I can with some confidence affirm, and say, That there cannot be a better Means used to teach it, nor a better Form to describe it. Which *Trill* and *Grup*, because they are a Step necessary unto many things that are describ'd, and are effects of that Grace which is most desired for Singing well; and (as is aforesaid) being described in one or other manner, do work a contrary effect to that which is requisite; I will shew, not only how they may be used, but also all the effects of them described in two manners, with the same value of the Notes, that still we may know, (as is aforementioned) that by these Writings, together with Practice, may be learned all the Curiosities of this Art.

Example of the most usual Graces.

1 Beating of the Throat.
2 Beating the Throat.
2 Trill.
2 Trill.
1 A plain fall.
2 Double fall.
A fall to take breath
Another fall like it.
Where this Mark + is set over a Note, the Trill is to be used.

It

It is to be obſerved in theſe Graces, that the ſecond hath more Grace in it than the firſt; and for your better Experience, we will in this following *Ayre* deſcribe ſome of thoſe Graces with Words under, together with the *Baſs* for the *Theorbo*; in which *Ayre* is contained the moſt Paſſionate Paſſages.

Abating the Voice.
A ſprightful Exclamation.
A more lively Exclam.
Deh deh doue ſon fuggiti deh doue ſon ſpariti
Exclam.
Excla. Excla.
Trillo.
gl'oc chi de qua-li-er rai I-o ſon cener homa i
Exclamation without meaſure, as it were Talking in Harmony, and neglecting the Muſick.
Aure Aure divine ch'er rate peregrine in queſta

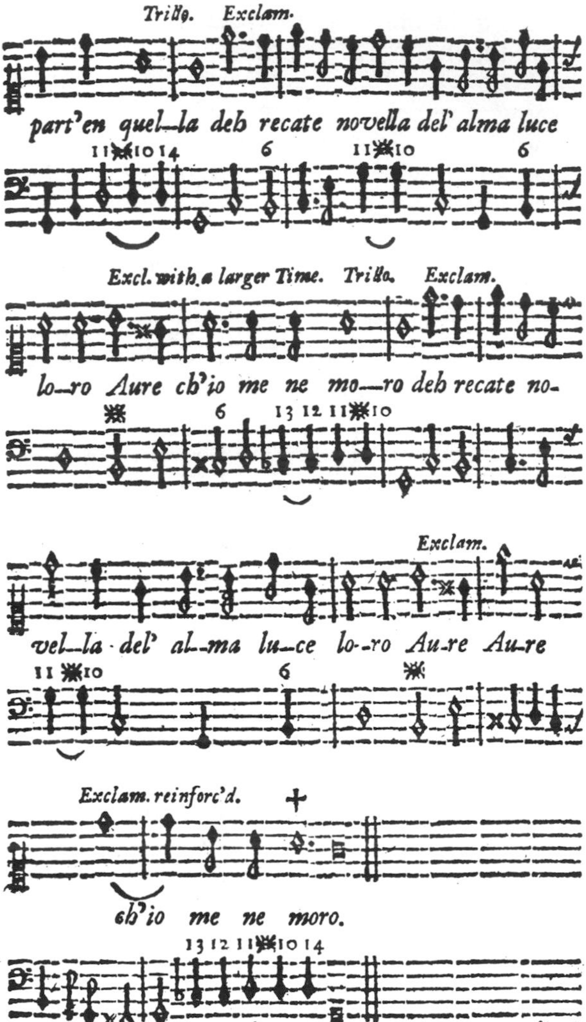
Trillo. Exclam.
part'en quel-la deh recate novella del' alma luce
11 10 14 6 11 10 6
Excl. with a larger Time. Trillo. Exclam.
lo-ro Aure ch'io me ne mo-ro deh recate no-
6 13 12 11 10
Exclam.
vel-la del' al-ma lu-ce lo-ro Au-re Au-re
11 10 6
Exclam. reinforc'd.
ch'io me ne moro.
13 12 11 10 14

And

And because in the two last Lines of the foregoing Ayre, *De doue son fuggiti,* there are contained the best Passions that can be used in this Noble manner of Singing, I have therefore thought good to set them down, both to shew where it is fit to encrease and abate the Voice, to make *Exclamations, Trills,* and *Grups;* and in a word, all the Treasures of this Art: And that they may serve for Example, whereby men may take notice in the Musick of the places, where they are most necessary, according to the Passions of the Words. Although I call that the *Noble manner of Singing,* which is used without tying a man's self to the ordinary measure of Time, making many times the Value of the Notes less by half, and sometimes more, according to the conceit of the words; whence proceeds that excellent kind of Singing with a graceful Neglect, whereof I have spoken before.

[" *Our Author having briefly set forth this chief " or most usual Grace in Singing called the* Trill, " *which (as he saith very right) is by a beating in the " Throat on the Vowel* [ah]; *some observe, that it is " rather the shaking of the* Uvula *or Pallate on the " Throat in one sound upon a Note. For the attain- " ing of this, the most surest and ready way is by imi- " tation of those who are perfect in the same; yet I " have heard of some that have attained it after this " manner: In the singing a plain Song of 6 Notes up " and 6 down, they have in the midst of every Note " beat or shaked with their Finger upon their Throat, " which by often practice came to do the same Notes " exactly without. It was also my chance to be in*

" *com-*

" *company with some Gentlemen at a Musical Practice,*
" *which sung their Parts very well, and used this Grace*
" *(called the* Trill) *very exactly: I desired to know*
" *their Tutor; they told me, I was their Tutor, for*
" *they never had any other but this my* Introdu-
" ction: *That (I answered) could direct them but in*
" *the Theory, they must needs have a better help in the*
" *Practick, especially in attaining to sing the* Trill
" *so well. One of them made this Reply; (which made*
" *me smile) I used,* said he, *at my first learning the*
" Trill, *to imitate that breaking of a Sound in the*
" *Throat which Men use when they Lewer their*
" *Hawks, as* He-he-he-he-he; *which he used slow*
" *at first, and after more swift on several Notes, higher*
" *and lower in sound, 'till he became perfect therein.*

" *The* Trill *being the most usual Grace, is usually*
" *made in* Closes, Cadences; *and when on a long*
" *Note* Exclamation *or* Passion *is expressed, there*
" *the* Trill *is made in the latter part of such Note;*
" *but most usually upon binding Notes, and such Notes*
" *as precede the closing Note. Those who once attain*
" *to the perfect uso of the* Trill, *other Graces will*
" *become easie.*]

Since then there are so many Effects to be used for the excellency of this Art, there is required (for the performing of them) necessarily a good Voice, as also good Wind to give liberty, and serve upon all occasions where is most need. It shall therefore be a profitable Advertisement, that the Professor of this Art, being to sing to a *Theorbo*, or other Stringed Instrument, and not being compelled

pelled to fit himſelf to others, that he ſo pitch his Tune, as to ſing his clear and natural Voice, avoiding feigned Tunes of Notes. In which, to feign them, or at the leaſt to inforce Notes, if his Wind ſerve him well, ſo as he do not diſcover them much, (becauſe for the moſt part they offend the Ear;) yet a Man muſt have a command of Breath to give the greater Spirit to the increaſing and diminiſhing of the Voice to *Exclamations* and other Paſſions as is related; therefore let him take heed, that ſpending much Breath upon ſuch Notes, it do not afterward fail him in ſuch places as it is moſt needful: For from a feigned Voice can come no noble manner of Singing, which only proceeds from a natural Voice, ſerving aptly for all the Notes which a Man can manage according to his Ability, employing his Wind in ſuch a faſhion as he commands all the beſt paſſionate Graces uſed in this moſt worthy manner of Singing. The love whereof, and generally of all Muſick, being kindled in me by a natural inclination, and by the ſtudy of ſo many years, ſhall excuſe me, if I have ſuffered my ſelf to be carried further than perhaps was fit for him, who no leſs eſteems and deſires to learn from others, than to communicate to others what himſelf hath learned; and to be further tranſported in this Diſcourſe, than can ſtand with that reſpect I bear to all the Profeſſors of this Art. Which Art being excellent, and naturally delightful, doth then become admirable, and entirely wins the love of others, when ſuch as poſſeſs it, both by teaching and delighting others, do often exerciſe it, and make it appear to be a Pattern and true Reſemblance of

thoſe

those never ceasing *Cælestial Harmonies*, whence proceed so many good Effects and Benefits upon Earth, raising and exciting the Minds of the Hearers to the Contemplation of those infinite Delights which Heaven affordeth.

Vale.

Several TUNES *of the most usual* PSALMS *Sung in Parish-Churches, with the* Bass *under each* Tune.

Psalm 4. Oxford Tune.

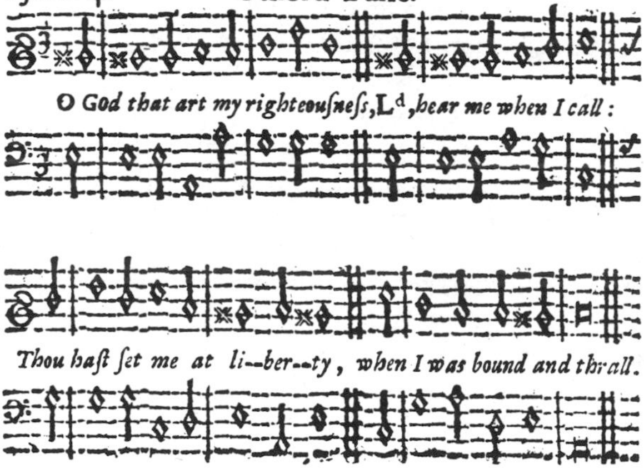
O God that art my righteousness, Ld, hear me when I call:
Thou hast set me at li--ber--ty, when I was bound and thrall.

Psalm 31. Lichfield Tune.

O Lord, I put my trust in thee, let nothing work me shame :

As thou art just, de-li-ver me, and set me quite from blame.

Psalm 34. Martyrs Tune.

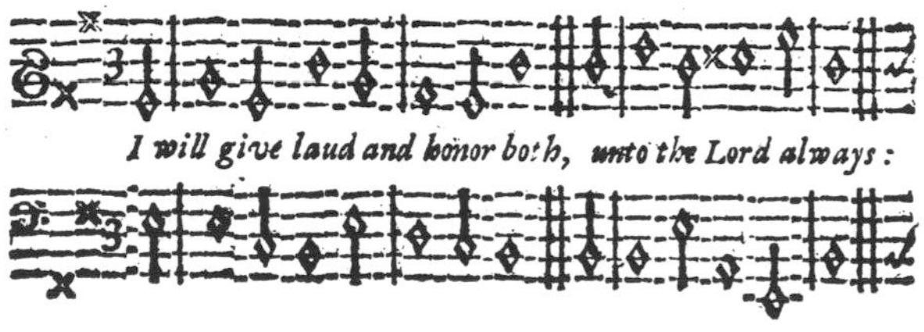
I will give laud and honor both, unto the Lord always :

And eke my mouth for evermore, shall speak un-to his praise.

Psalm 23. Canterbury Tune.

The Lord is on-ly my ſupport, and he that doth me feed:
How can I then lack a--ny thing, whereof I ſtand in need?

Psalm 25, 50, 67, 70, or 134. Southwel Tune.

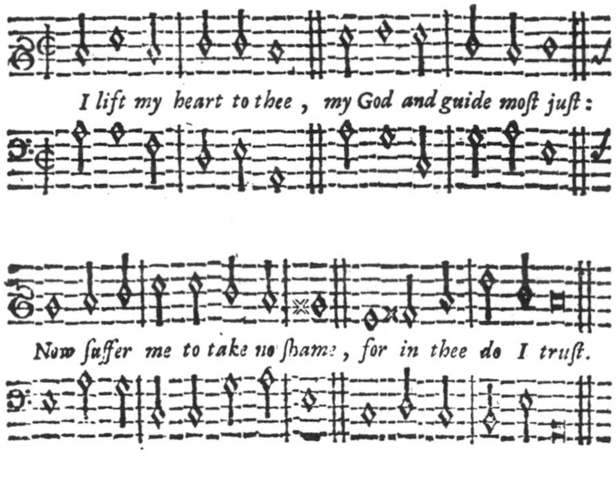
I lift my heart to thee, my God and guide moſt juſt:
Now ſuffer me to take no ſhame, for in thee do I truſt.

Psalm 78. York Tune.

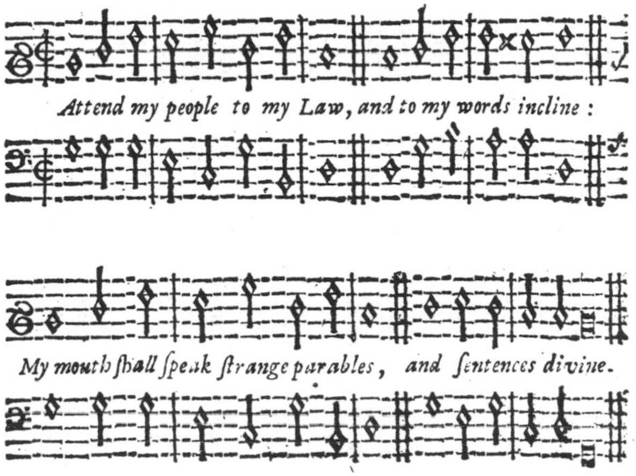
Attend my people to my Law, and to my words incline:
My mouth ſhall ſpeak ſtrange parables, and ſentences divine.

Psalm 91. St. Mary's Tune.

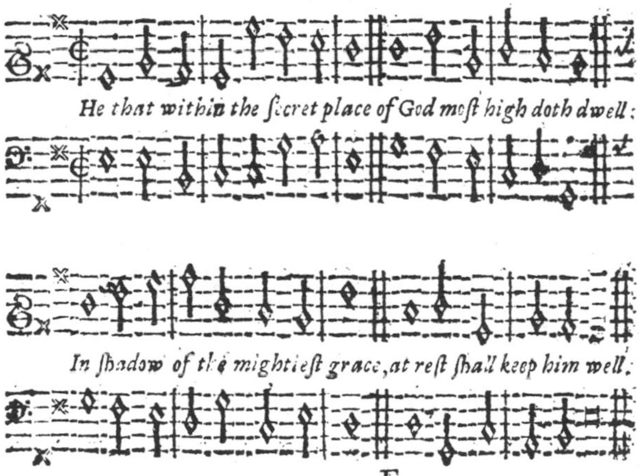
He that within the ſecret place of God moſt high doth dwell:
In ſhadow of the mightieſt grace, at reſt ſhall keep him well.

Psalm 95. St. David's Tune.

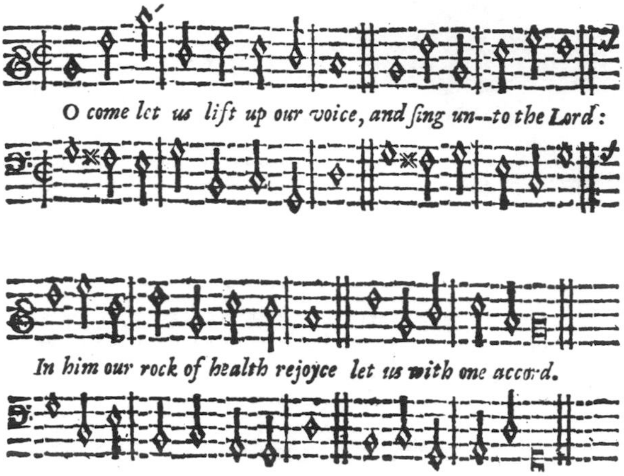
O come let us lift up our voice, and sing un--to the Lord:
In him our rock of health rejoyce let us with one accord.

Psalm 100. Proper Tune.

All people yt on earth do dwell, sing to th: L. with chearful voice:
Him serve wth fear, his praise forth tel, com ye before him, & rejoice.

Psalm 119. Proper Tune.

Blessed are they that perfect are, and pure in mind and heart:
Whose lives and con-ver-sa-ti-ons from God's laws never start.
Blessed are they that give themselves his statutes to observe:
Seeking the L. with all their heart, & ne-ver from him swerve.

Psalm 113. Proper Tune.

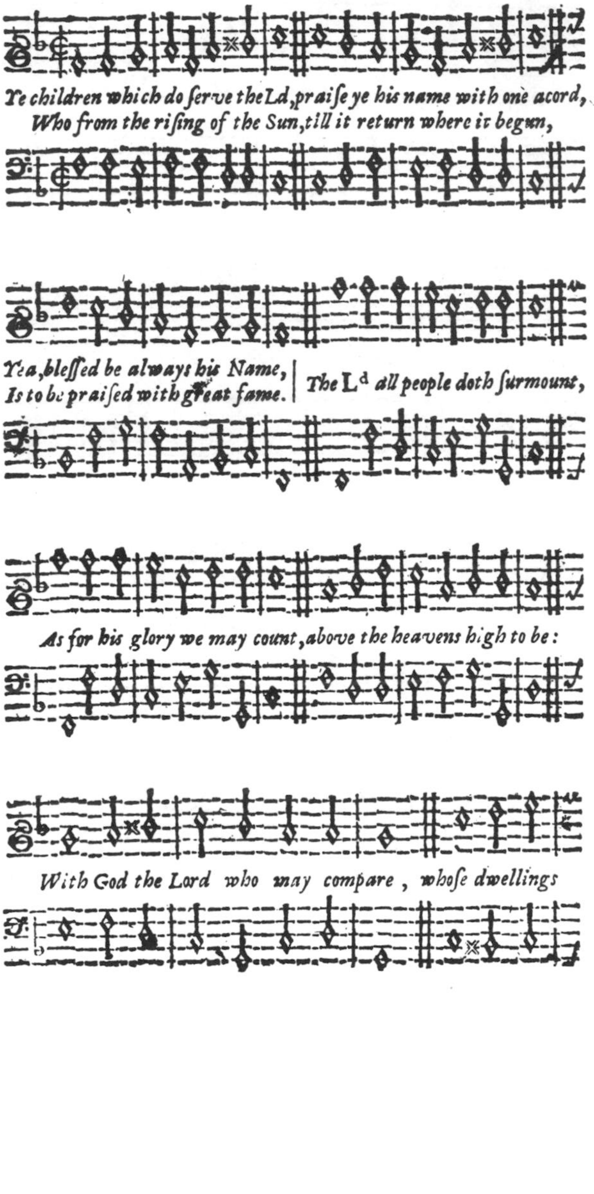
Ye children which do serve the Ld, praise ye his name with one acord,
Who from the rising of the Sun, till it return where it begun,
Yea, blessed be always his Name,
Is to be praised with great fame.
The Ld all people doth surmount,
As for his glory we may count, above the heavens high to be:
With God the Lord who may compare, whose dwellings

in the heavens are? Of such great pow'r and force is hs.

Psalm 148. Proper Tune.

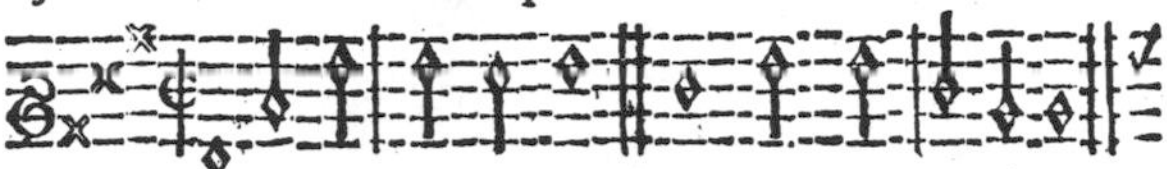

Give laud unto the Lord, from heav'n that is so high:

Praise him in deed and word, above the starry sky: And also ye,

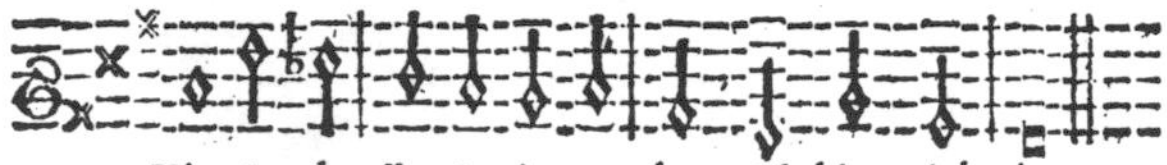

His Angels all, Armies royal, praise him with gl.e.

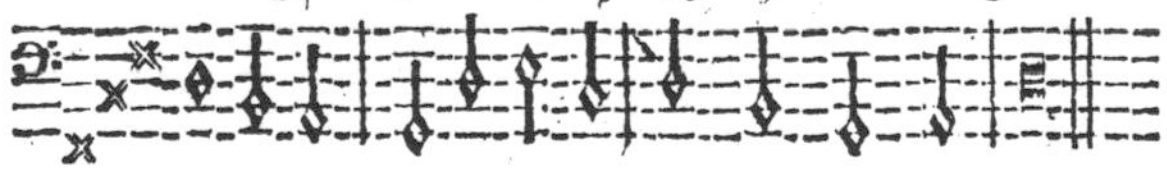

☞ The whole Book of *Psalms* and *Hymns* are Printed in a Pocket Volume, with the Tunes to each Psalm in Three Parts, *Cantus*, *Medius*, and *Bassus*, in a more plain and easie Method than any heretofore Printed; to which (when you are perfect in these) I refer you.

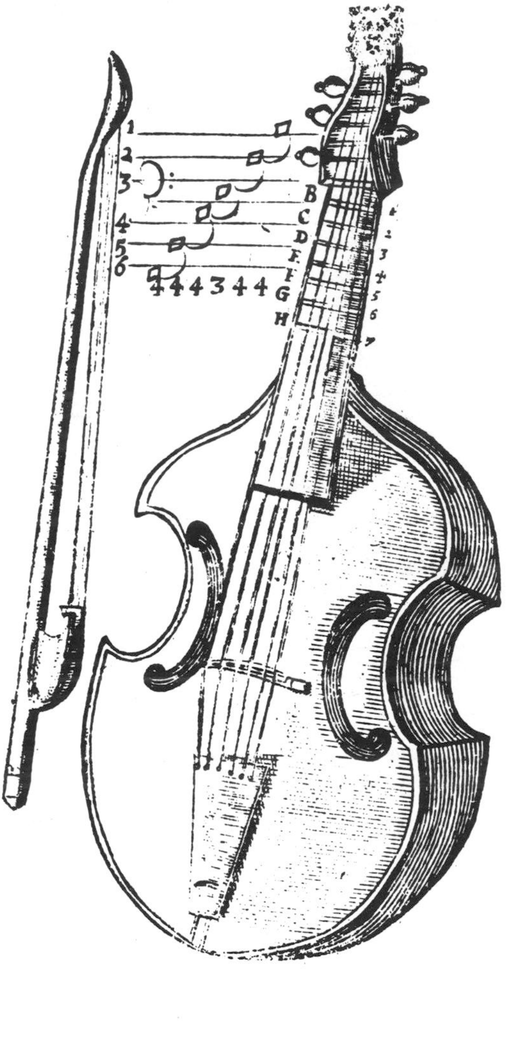
1
2
3
4
5
6
B
C
D
E
F
G
H
4 4 4 3 4 4

A BRIEF INTRODUCTION To the Playing on the Bass-Viol.

The Second BOOK.

THIS *Viol* is usually called *de Gambo*, or the *Bass* or *Consort-Viol*, because the Musick thereon is played from the Rules of the *Gam-ut*, and not as the *Lyra-Viol*, which is by Letters or Tablature. Of this *Viol de Gambo*, there are three several sizes, one larger than the other, according to the three Parts of *Musick* set forth in the *Gam-ut*, viz. *Treble-Viol*, *Tenor-Viol*, and *Bass-Viol*. The *Treble-Viol* plays the highest Part, and its Lessons are prick'd by the *G sol re ut* Cliff 𝄞; the *Tenor-Viol*, or middle Part, its Lessons are by the *C sol fa ut* Cliff 𝄡; and the *Bass-Viol*, which is the largest, its Lessons are by the *F fa ut* Cliff 𝄢. Theſe three *Viols* agree in one manner of Tuning; therefore I ſhall firſt give you Directions for Tuning the *Baſs-Viol*, which is uſually ſtrung with *Six Strings*, (as you may obſerve on the Figure expreſſed in the foregoing Page,) which ſix Strings are known by ſix ſeveral Names: The *firſt*, which is the ſmalleſt, is called the *Treble*; the *ſecond*, the *Small Mean*; the *third*, the *Great Mean*; the *fourth*, the *Counter-Tenor*; the *fifth*, the *Tenor* or *Gam-ut* String; the *ſixth*, the *Baſs*. But if you will Name them after they are Tuned, according to the Rule of the *Gam-ut*, the *Treble* String is *D la ſol re*; the *Small Mean*, *A la mi re*; the *Great Mean*, *E la mi*; the *Counter-Tenor*, *C fa ut*; the *Tenor* or fifth String, *Gam-ut*; and the ſixth or *Baſs*, Double *D ſol re*. Belonging to theſe *ſix Strings* there are *ſeven Frets* or *Stops* on the *Neck* of the *Viol*, which are put for ſtopping the various Sounds according to the ſeveral Notes of the *Gam-ut*, both *Flat* and *Sharp*: For the more plain underſtanding of which, I have drawn an exact *Table* in Page 60, and 61, beginning with the loweſt *Note* on the *ſixth String*, and ſo aſcending to the higheſt on the *firſt* or *Treble String*. The perfect underſtanding of which Table, will much further you in the knowledge of Tuning the *Viol*; for which Tuning, I will give two *Rules*, one by *Tablature* or *Letters*, the other by the *Gam-ut* Rule: The firſt being the eaſieſt way to a Beginner, whoſe Ear at firſt being not well acquainted with the exact Diſtances of Sounds the Strings are Tuned in, may by this way uſe only one Sound, *viz.* an *Uniſon*, which is to make two Strings (one of them being ſtopt,

the

the other not) to agree in the ſame Sound: The Letters are Eight, *A*, *B*, *C*, *D*, *E*, *F*, *G*, *H*; ſeven of theſe are aſſigned to the ſeven *Frets* on the Neck of the *Viol*: *A* is for the String open, *B* is the firſt Fret, *C* the ſecond, *D* the third, *E* the fourth, *F* the fifth, *G* the ſixth, and *H* the ſeventh.

Example.

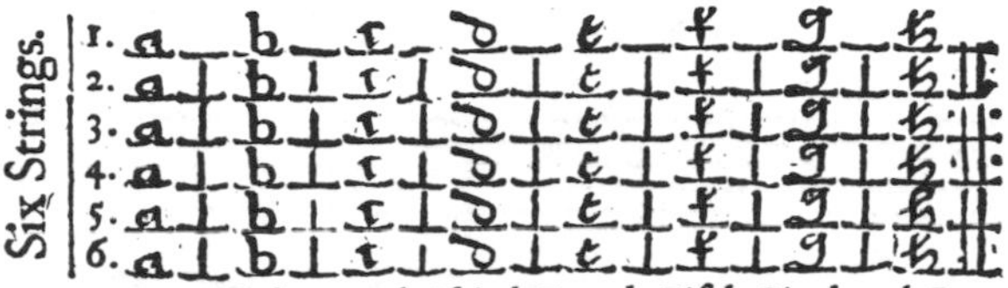
Six Strings.
1.
2.
3.
4.
5.
6.

Open. Firſt, Second, Third, Fourth, Fifth, Sixth, 7th Fret.

When you begin to Tune, raiſe your *Treble* or ſmalleſt String as high as conveniently it will bear without breaking; then ſtop only your *Second* or *Small Mean* in *F*, and Tune it till it agree in *Uniſon* with your *Treble* open; that done, ſtop your *Third* in *F*, and make it agree with your *Second* open; then ſtop your *Fourth* in *E*, and make it agree with your *Third* open; then ſtop your *Fifth* in *F*, and make it agree with your *Fourth* open; and laſtly, ſtop your *Sixth* in *F*, and make it agree to your *Fifth* open. This being exactly done, you will find your *Viol* in Tune, according to the *Rule* of the *Gam-ut*.

Ex-

Example of Tuning by Letters.

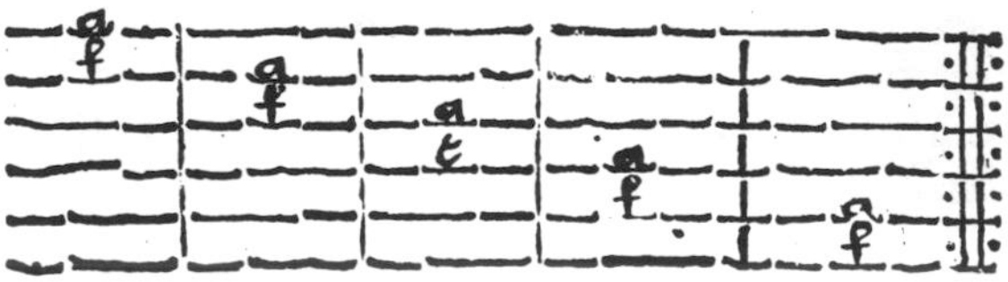

Example of Tuning by Notes.

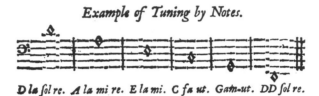

D la sol re. A la mi re. E la mi. C fa ut. Gam-ut. DD sol re.

The other way of *Tuning* is by the Rule of the *Gam-ut*, by diſtances of *Sounds*, as in the foregoing Example, thus: The *Treble* being raiſed as high as it will conveniently bear without breaking, is called *D la ſol re*; then Tune your *Second* four Notes lower, and it is *A la mi re*; the *Third* four Notes lower, is *E la mi*; the *Fourth* three Notes, or a flat *Third* lower, is *C fa ut*; the *Fifth* four Notes lower, is *Gam-ut*; and the *Sixth* four Notes lower than the *Fifth*, is Double *D ſol re*. This is the moſt uſual way of Tuning it; yet there are ſome Leſſons do require it one Note lower, which is Double *C fa ut*, but that is very ſeldom.

Exam-

Example of the NOTES *ascending and descending by* Tablature *and* Notes, *as they ascend and descend on the several Frets or Stops.*

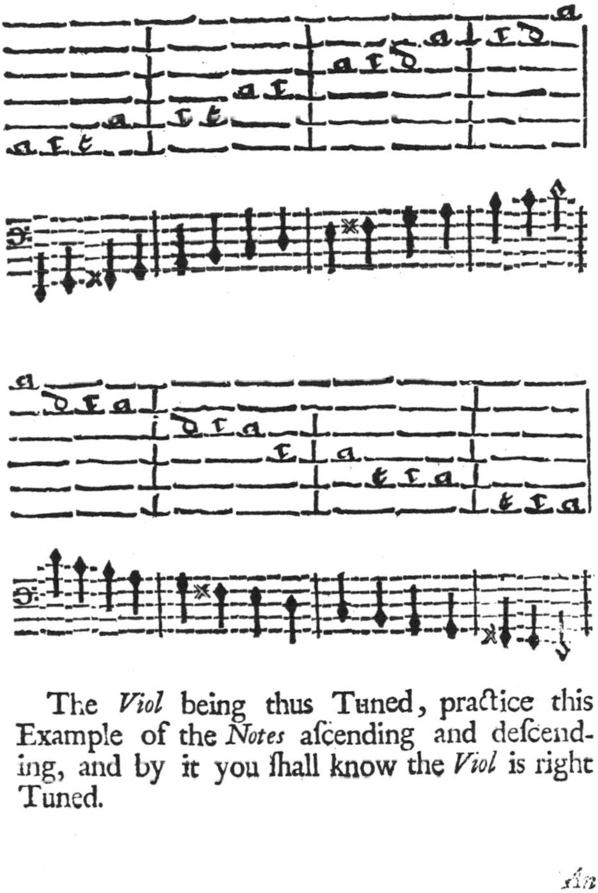

The *Viol* being thus Tuned, practice this Example of the *Notes* ascending and descending, and by it you shall know the *Viol* is right Tuned.

An exact TABLE, *directing the Places of all the* Notes, *flat and ſharp, to every Stop on the* Baſs-Viol, *according to the* Gam-ut, *beginning at the loweſt Note of the* Baſs *on the* Sixth String, *and aſcending to the higheſt on the* Treble *or* Firſt String.

Sixth String.

Open. First Fret. 2d Fret. 3d Fret. 4th Fret.

Double D ſol re. DD E la mi, flat. *DD E la mi,* proper. *DD F fa ut. DD F fa ut,* ſharp.

Fifth String.

Open. Firſt Fret. 2d Fret. 3d Fret. 4th Fret.

Gam-ut. Gam-ut ſharp. *A re. B mi* flat. *B mi* proper.

Fourth String.

Open. Firſt Fret. 2d Fret. 3d Fret.

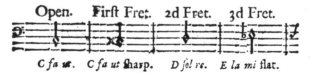

C fa ut. C fa ut ſharp. *D ſol re. E la mi* flat.

Third

Third String.

Open. First Fret. 2d Fret. 3d Fret. 4th Fret.

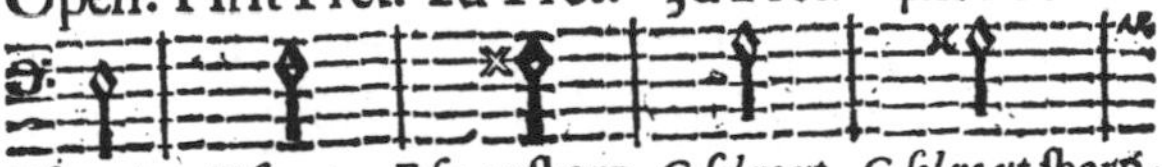

E la mi. *F fa ut.* *F fa ut* sharp. *G sol re ut.* *G sol re ut* sharp.

Second String.

Open. First Fret. 2d Fret. 3d Fret. 4th Fret.

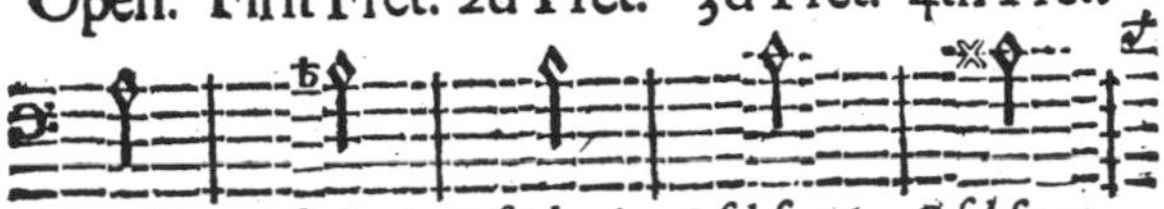

A la mi re. *B fa b mi,* flat. *B fa b mi,* proper. *C sol fa ut.* *C sol fa ut,* sharp.

First String.

Open. First Fret. 2d Fret. 3d Fret. 4th Fret. 5th Fret.

D la sol re. *E la mi* flat. *E la mi.* *F fa ut.* *F fa ut* sharp. *G sol re ut.*

It is usual in Lessons for the *Bass-Viol,* to add a *Sixth Line* above or below if the Note require, or to change the *Cliff* when the Notes ascend above *D la sol re;* the Practitioner ought therefore to be perfect in the *C sol fa ut* Cliff on the middle Line, as you see in the five last Notes of the *Table:* Also this Example mentions the Agreement of Notes in both Cliffs, *Bass* and *Tenor.*

Example

Example.

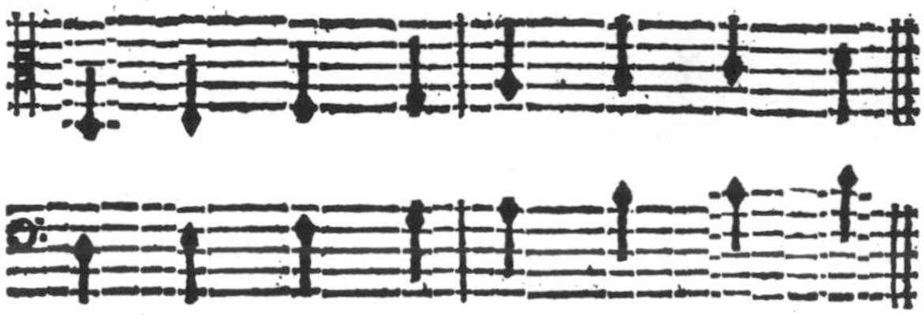

In this Example, the *Notes* prick'd in the *Tenor* Cliff are the ſame with thoſe in the *Baſs* or *F fa ut* Cliff, and are ſtopp'd in the ſame places on the *Viol.* This I thought fit to mention, becauſe you will meet with the change of *Cliffs* in ſome of the following Leſſons. Next

Obſerve, That in the foregoing Table the (✻) *Sharp* before a Note makes it ſtopp'd a *Fret* lower, and a (♭) *Flat* before a Note makes it ſtopp'd a *Fret* higher; for two *Frets* go to one whole or perfect *Note*, as that Table doth direct. Sometimes you may ſee a *Sharp* before *D ſol re*, then it is ſtopp'd a *Fret* lower, which is the place of *E la mi* flat; ſo if a *Flat* be ſet before *A la mi re*, it is ſtopp'd a *Fret* higher, which is *G ſol re ut* ſharp. The like of other *flat* or *ſharp* Notes.

Alſo, if a *B flat* or *B ſharp* be ſet on *Rule* or *Space* at the beginning of any Line with the *Cliff*, that *Flat* or *Sharp* makes all the Notes which are in the ſame Rules or Spaces to be *flat* or *ſharp* through the whole Leſſon.

Treble.

Treble-Viol.

These *Directions* for the *Bass-Viol* do also serve the *Treble-Viol,* which is strung with six Strings, and Tuned in the same manner, only eight Notes higher: *G sol re ut* on the *Treble* is the Eighth above *G sol re ut* on the *Bass*, being stopp'd on the same *String* and *Fret* with the *Bass*; and so other Notes accordingly.

Example of Tuning.

1 String. 2 String. 3 String. 4 String. 5 String. 6 String.

D la sol. A la mi re. E la mi. C sol fa ut. G sol re ut. D la sol re.

Tenor-Viol.

The *Tenor-Viol* is an excellent *Inward Part*, and much used in *Consort*, especially in *Phantasies* and *Ayres* of 3, 4, 5, and 6 Parts. The Tuning of it is the same with the *Bass* and *Treble* for the distance of *sound* betwixt each String; but being an *Inward Part* betwixt both, its Tuning is four Notes higher than the *Bass*, and five Notes lower than the *Treble*; its *First* or *Treble String* is Tuned to *G sol re ut* on the third String of the *Treble-Viol*; its *second* four Notes lower, which is *D la sol re*; the *third* four Notes lower, is *A la mi re*; the *fourth* three Notes (or a flat *Third*) lower, is *F fa ut*; the

fifth

fifth four Notes lower than it, is *C fa ut*; and the *ſixth* four Notes lower than the *fifth*, is *Gam-ut*; which is anſwerable to the *Gam-ut* on the *Baſs-Viol*.

Example.

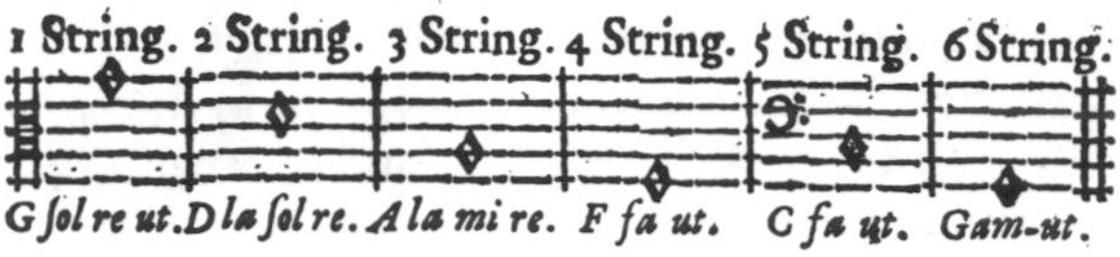
1 String. 2 String. 3 String. 4 String. 5 String. 6 String.
G ſol re ut. D la ſol re. A la mi re. F fa ut. C fa ut. Gam-ut.

Some General Rules *for the* Viol.

THere are *three ſorts* of *BASS-VIOLS*, as there are three manner of ways in Playing.

1. A *Baſs-Viol* for *Conſort* muſt be one of the largeſt ſize, and the Strings proportionable.

2. A *Baſs-Viol* for *Diviſions* muſt be of a leſs ſize, and the Strings according.

3. A *Baſs-Viol* to Play *Lyra-way*, that is, by *Tablature*, muſt be ſomewhat leſs than the two former, and Strung proportionably.

4. In the choice of your *Viol-Bow*, let it be proportioned to the *Viol* you uſe; and let the Hair be laid ſtiff, and the *Bow* not too heavy, nor too long.

5. In holding your *Viol*, obſerve this *Rule*: Place it gently between your Knees, reſting the lower end thereof upon the Calves of your Legs, and let your Feet reſt flat on the Ground, your Toes turned a little outward, and let the top of your *Viol* lean towards your left Shoulder.

6. In

6. In holding of your Bow, obſerve this *Rule*: Hold the Bow betwixt the ends of your Thumb and Fore Finger an Inch below the Nut, the Thumb and Fore Finger reſting on the Wood, the ends of your ſecond and third Fingers ſtay'd upon the Hair, by which you may poiſe and keep up your Bow. Your Bow being thus fixed, you muſt draw it over one String, and then over another, in a Right-Angle, about 2 or 3 inches above the Bridge, making each ſeveral String yield a clear ſound without touching the other.

7. In the Poſture of your left Hand obſerve this *Rule*: Place your Thumb on the back of the Neck, and oppoſite to your Fore Finger, ſo that when your Fingers are to reſt on the ſeveral Stops or Frets, your hand may have liberty to move up and down as occaſion ſhall require. And in the ſtopping obſerve, That when you ſet any Finger down, let it not be juſt upon the Fret, but cloſe to it, bearing it hard down to the end of your Finger, and let it reſt there until occaſion require the moving it; and be ſure not to lift your Fingers too high, but keep them in an even diſtance to the Frets, that ſo they may paſs more readily from Fret to Fret.

8. In the Rule of true *Fingering*, where you skip a Fret, there leave a Finger; and when you have any Notes which are high Notes, that go lower than the Frets, there thoſe higheſt Notes are always ſtopp'd either with the third or fourth Finger, (by ſhifting the Fingers lower;) if with the third, then the firſt and ſecond Fingers are ready to ſtop the two next Notes either aſcending or deſcending from it: But if the higheſt Note be ſtopp'd with

the ſourth Finger, then the Note under it is ſtopp'd either with the third or ſecond Finger, according as it is either *Flat* or *Sharp*; if *Sharp*, the third; if *Flat*, the ſecond. But whether the higheſt Note be ſtopp'd with the third or fourth Finger, the third below it muſt be ſtopp'd with the firſt Finger, which is ever as a *Guide* to the two Notes above it. Laſtly, when two Notes which follow one another are ſtopp'd with the ſame Finger removed, it is to prepare the other Fingers to the fore-mentioned Poſture, or to remove them to ſome other place. This order of *Fingering* directs the whole Finger-board, (in ſtopping three Notes which follow upon any one ſtring,) with this *Proviſo*; Where Stops are wide, the fourth or little Finger is of more uſe when lower down, where the Stops fall more cloſe.

9. In the moving your *Bow*, obſerve this *Rule*: When you ſee an even number of *Quavers* or *Semiquavers*, as 2, 4, 6, or 8, tied together, you muſt begin with your *Bow* forward, though the *Bow* be drawn forward the Note before; but if the Number be odd, as 3, 5, or 7, (which is by reaſon of a *Prick'd Note*, or an odd *Quaver Reſt*) then the firſt Note muſt be Play'd with the *Bow* drawn backward.

Laſtly, in the Practice of any Leſſon, Play it ſlow at firſt, and by often Practice it will bring your Hand to a more ſwift motion.

And now your *VIOL* being Tuned according to the foregoing Directions, I have here following ſet down a few *Leſſons* for to begin with; and over the *Notes* I have ſet Figures, to direct with what

what *Fingers* to ſtop them; 1, 2, 3, 4, is ſet for *firſt*, *ſecond*, *third*, and *fourth Fingers*; thoſe which have no *Figures* over them, are the Strings open.

For the uſual *Graces*, the *Shake* is the principal; of which there are two, the *Cloſe Shake*, and the *Open Shake*; the *Cloſe Shake* is, when you ſtop with your firſt Finger on the firſt Fret, and *ſhake* with your ſecond Finger as cloſe to it as you can; the *Open Shake* is, when you ſtop with your firſt Finger on the firſt Fret, and *ſhake* with your third Finger on the third Fret: Third obſerve in all Stops whatſoever. For other *Graces*, as *Double-Reliſhes*, *Backfalls*, &c. I refer you to the *Table of the ſeveral Graces* in my *Directions* for the *Treble-Violin*, which are proper alſo to the *Baſs-Viol*.

Short LESSONS *for the* Baſs-Viol.

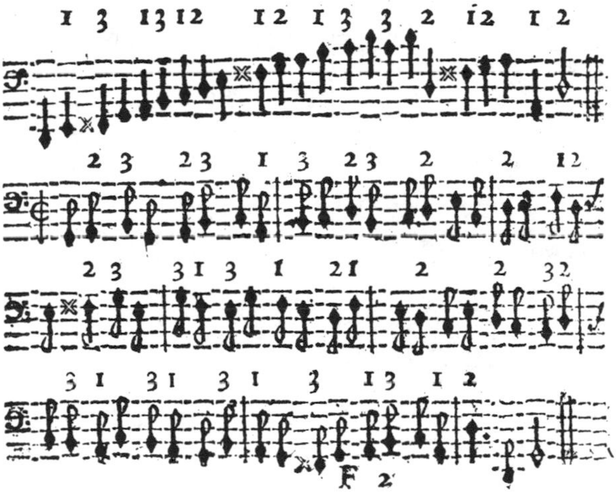

A Division on a Ground.

A Ground.
A Ground.
A Ground.
A Tune.

A Tune.
A Preludium.

A BRIEF

A BRIEF INTRODUCTION To the Playing on the Treble-Violin.

THE *Treble-Violin* is a chearful and spritely Instrument, and much practised of late, some by Book, and some without; which of these two is the best way, may easily be resolved: To learn to Play by *Rote* or *Ear*, without Book, is the way never to Play more than what may be gain'd by hearing another Play which may soon be forgot; but on the contrary, he which

Learns and Practiſes by Book according to the *Gam-ut*, (which is the *True Rule* for Muſick) fails not, after he comes to be Perfect in thoſe *Rules*, which guide him to Play more than ever he was taught or heard, and alſo to Play his Part in *Conſort*, which the other can never be capable of.

Directions for Tuning *the* Violin.

THE *Violin* is uſually ſtrung with *four Strings*, and Tuned by *Fifths*: For the more plain and eaſie underſtanding thereof, and ſtopping all *Notes* in their right *Places* and *Tune*, it will be neceſſary, That on the *Neck* or *Finger-board* of your *Violin* there be placed *ſix Frets* as is on a *Viol*: This tho' it be not uſual, yet it is the beſt and eaſieſt way for a Beginner who has a bad Ear; for by thoſe Frets he has a certain *Rule* to direct and guide him to ſtop all his *Notes* in exact *Tune*; whereas thoſe that Learn without, ſeldom have at firſt ſo good an Ear to ſtop all *Notes* in perfect *Tune*. Therefore for the better underſtanding thereof, in this following *Example* is aſſigned to thoſe *ſix Frets* on the *Finger-board*, ſix *Letters* of the Alphabet in their order: The firſt *Fret* is *B*, the ſecond *C*, the third *D*, the fourth *E*, the fifth *F*, and the ſixth *G*. *A* is not aſſigned to any *Fret*, but is the String open.

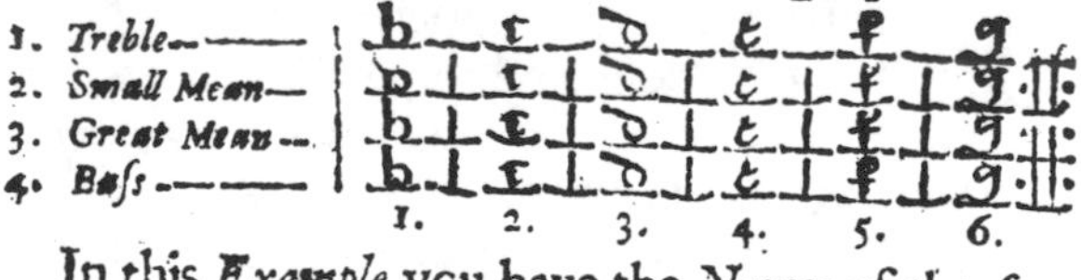
1. Treble
2. Small Mean
3. Great Mean
4. Baſs
b c d e f g
1. 2. 3. 4. 5. 6.

In this *Example* you have the *Names* of the *four Strings*, with the *Letters* aſſigned to each *Fret*.

The

The Scale *of* MUSICK *on the Four Strings of the* Treble-Violin, *expressed by* Letters *and* Notes.

First String, or *Treble.*

Second, or *Small Mean.*

Third, or *Great Mean.*

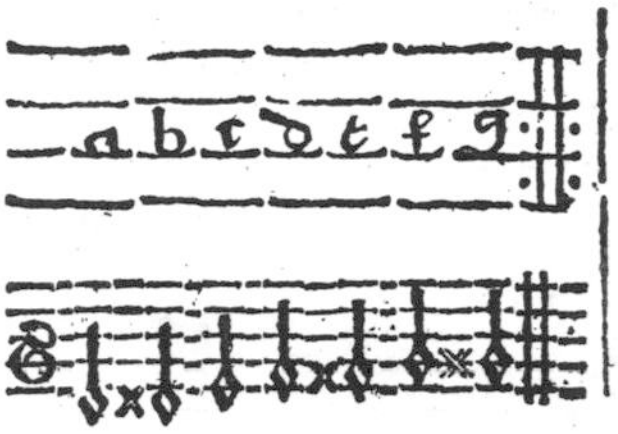

Fourth String, or *Bass.*

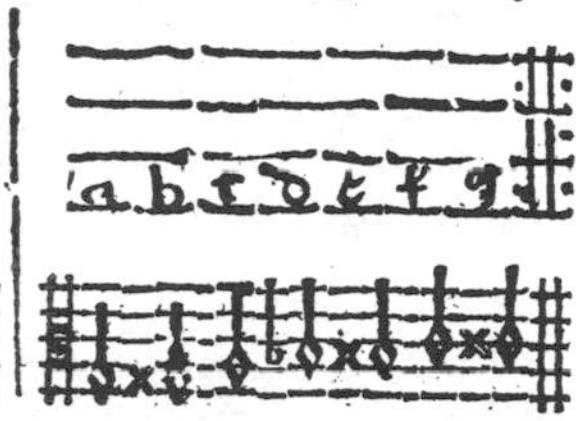

This Example doth direct the Places of all the *Notes* flat and sharp, each *Note* being placed under the *Letter*, according to their several *Stops* upon each *String* distinctly, beginning at the lowest *Note* on the *Bass* or *Fourth String*, and ascending up to the highest on the *Treble* or *First String*, according to the *Scale* of the *Gam-ut*: In which you may also observe, That the *Lessons* for the *Violin* by *Letters* are prick'd on *four Lines* according to the *four* several *Strings*; but *Lessons* by *Notes* are prick'd upon *five Lines*, as appears in that Example.

For

For the *Tuning* of the *Violin* is usually by *Fifths*, which is five Notes distance betwixt each *String*; which according to the *Scale* or *Gam-ut*, the *Bass* or *fourth String* is called G *sol re ut*; the *third* or *Great Mean*, *D la sol re*; the *second* or *Small Mean*, *A la mi re*; the *first* or *Treble*, E *la*; as in the following Example. The first *Note* of each *String* is upon a, and is known by this Signature * over each of those *Notes*.

Example of the Tuning *as the five Notes ascend on each of the four Strings, beginning on the* Bass *or fourth String.*

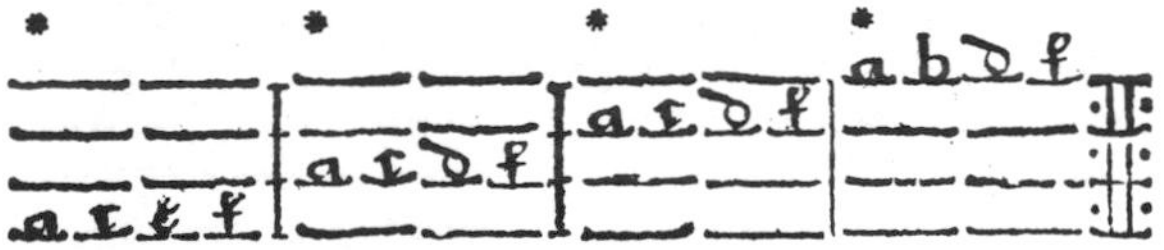

4th String. 3d String. 2d String. First String.

G sol re ut. D la sol re. A la mi re. E la.

Also, for a Beginner to Tune by *Eighths*, will be easier than by *Fifths*, if his *Violin* be *fretted*; to begin which, he must wind up his *first* or *Treble String* as high as it will bear, then *stop* it in *F*, and Tune his *second* an *Eighth* below it; then *stop* the *second* in F, and Tune the *third* an *Eighth* under it; then *stop* the *third* in F, and Tune the *fourth* an *Eighth* below that; and so your *Strings* will be in perfect Tune.

Exam-

Example of Tuning by Fifths *and* Eighths.

By Fifths. *By Eighths.*

1.
2.
3.
1.
2.
3.
2.
3.
4.
2.
3.
4.

Another Scale *for the* VIOLIN, *directing the Places of the* Notes *on each String, and the* Stops *by each Finger.*

First String.

Open. First Finger. 2d Finger. 3d Finger.

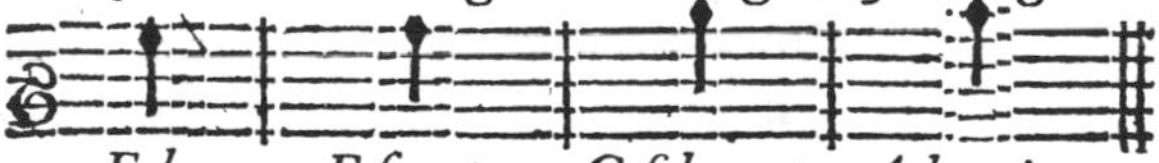

E la. F fa ut. G sol re ut. A la mi re.

Second String.

Open. First Finger. 2d Finger. 3d Finger.

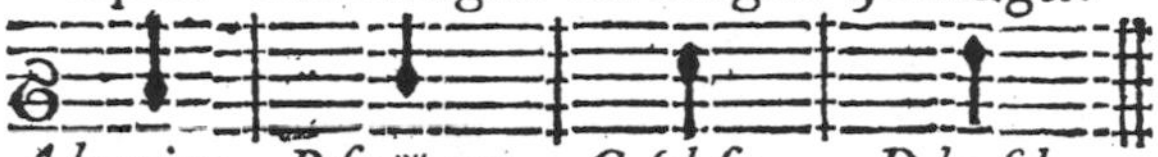

A la mi re. B fa ♮ mi. C sol fa. D la sol.

Third String.

Open. First Finger. 2d Finger. 3d Finger.

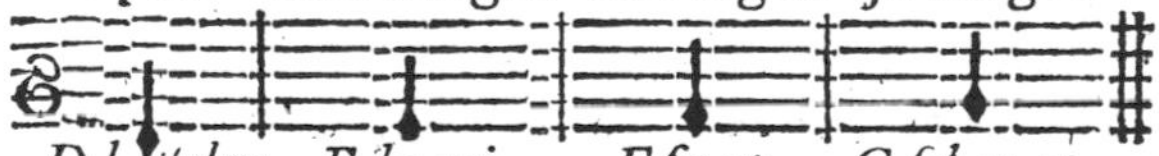

D la sol re. E la mi. F fa ut. G sol re ut.

Fourth String.

Open. First Finger. 2d Finger. 3d Finger.

G sol re ut. A la mi re. B fa b mi. C sol fa ut.

Having thus given you the *Tuning* of the *Treble-Violin*, it will be very neceſſary here to ſet down the Tuning of the *Tenor-Violin*, and the *Baſs-Violin*, being both uſed in Conſort. The *Tenor* or *Mean* is a larger *Violin* than the *Treble*, and is Tuned five Notes lower than the *Treble*; and the *Cliff* is put ſometimes on the middle, and ſometimes on the ſecond Line.

Example.

Tuning the **Tenor-Violin.**

First String. 2d String. 3d String. 4th String.

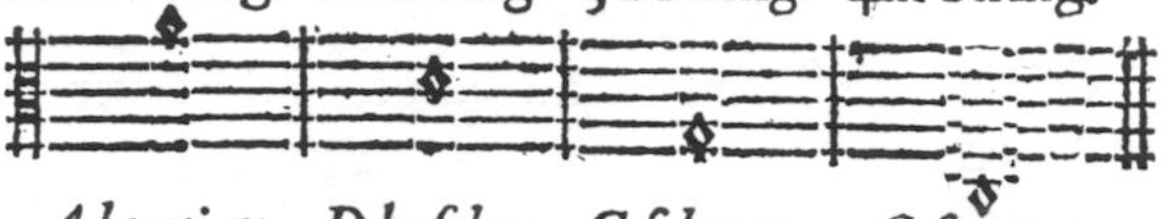

A la mi re. D la ſol re. G ſol re ut. C fa ut.

Tuning the **Baſs-Violin.**

First String. 2d String. 3d String. 4th String.

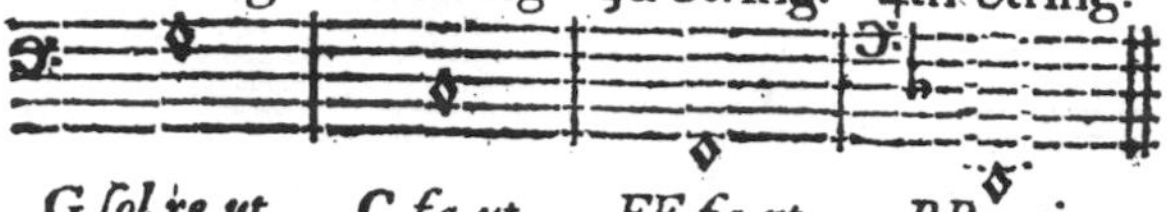

G ſol re ut. C fa ut. FF fa ut. BB mi.

Thus (after the plaineſt method I could) I have ſet down ſeveral *Rules* and *Directions* for the *Treble-Violin* by way of *Fretting*, which I have known uſed by ſome Eminent Teachers on this Inſtrument as the moſt facile and eaſie to Initiate their Scholars; and alſo *Directions* for Pricking down *Leſſons* in *Letters*; Yet I do not approve of this way of Playing by *Letters*, ſave only as a Guide to young Practitioners, to bring them the more

more readily to know all the Stops and Places of the *Notes* both *flat* and *sharp*, and being perfect therein, to lay the use of *Letters* aside, and keep to their Practice by *Notes* and *Rules* of the *Gam-ut* only: For this reason I have added some few *Lessons* both ways, that after you can play them by *Letters*, you may play the same again by *Notes*.

☞ *Those that desire more Lessons for this Instrument, may be furnished with them in the First and Second Parts of* Apollo's-Banquet, *lately Published, containing the newest Tunes for the* Violin, *with the most usual* French *Dances used at Court and Dancing-Schools. And in the Book called* The Dancing-Master, *lately Reprinted, with large Additions of the newest Tunes of Dances now in use.*

Some General Rules *for the* Treble-Violin.

FIrst, The *Violin* is usually Play'd above-hand, the Neck thereof being held by the left hand, the lower part thereof is rested on the left Breast, a little below the Shoulder: The *Bow* is held in the right Hand between the ends of the Thumb and three Fingers, the Thumb being stay'd upon the Hair at the Nut, and the three Fingers resting upon the Wood. Your *Bow* being thus fix'd, you are first to draw an *even stroak* over each *String* severally, making each *String* yield a clear and distinct sound.

Secondly, For the Posture of your left Hand, place your Thumb on the back of the Neck opposite to your fore Finger, so will your Fingers have the more liberty to move up and down on the several Stops.

Thirdly,

Thirdly, For true Fingering obſerve theſe Directions, (which will appear more eaſie to your underſtanding, if in your firſt Practice you have your *Violin* Fretted, as is before-mentioned,) That where you skip a *Fret* or *Stop*, there to leave a Finger, for every *Stop* is but half a Tone or Note; for from b to c is but half a Note, but from b to d is a whole Note; therefore the leaving of a Finger is neceſſary to be in readineſs when half Notes happen, which is by *Flats* and *Sharps*.

Fourthly, When you have any high Notes which reach lower than your uſual Frets or Stops, there you are to ſhift your Fingers; if there be but two Notes, then the firſt is ſtopp'd with the ſecond Finger, and the reſt by the next Fingers.

Fifthly, In the moving your *Bow* up and down, obſerve this Rule: When you ſee an *even Number* of *Quavers* and *Semiquavers*, as 2, 4, 6, or 8, tied together, your Bow muſt move up, tho' it was up at the Note immediately before; but if you have an *odd Number*, as 3, 5, or 7, (which happens very often by reaſon of a Prick'd *Note*, or an odd *Quaver* Reſt,) there your *Bow* muſt be drawn downwards at the firſt *Note*.

Laſtly, In your Practice of any Leſſon, play it ſlow at firſt, and by often Practice it will bring your Hand to a more ſwift motion.

As for the ſeveral *Graces* and *Flouriſhes* that are uſed, as *Shakes*, *Backfalls*, and *Double Reliſhes*, this following TABLE will be ſome help to your Practice; for there is, firſt, the *Note* plain; and after, the *Grace* expreſſed by *Notes* at length.

A Table

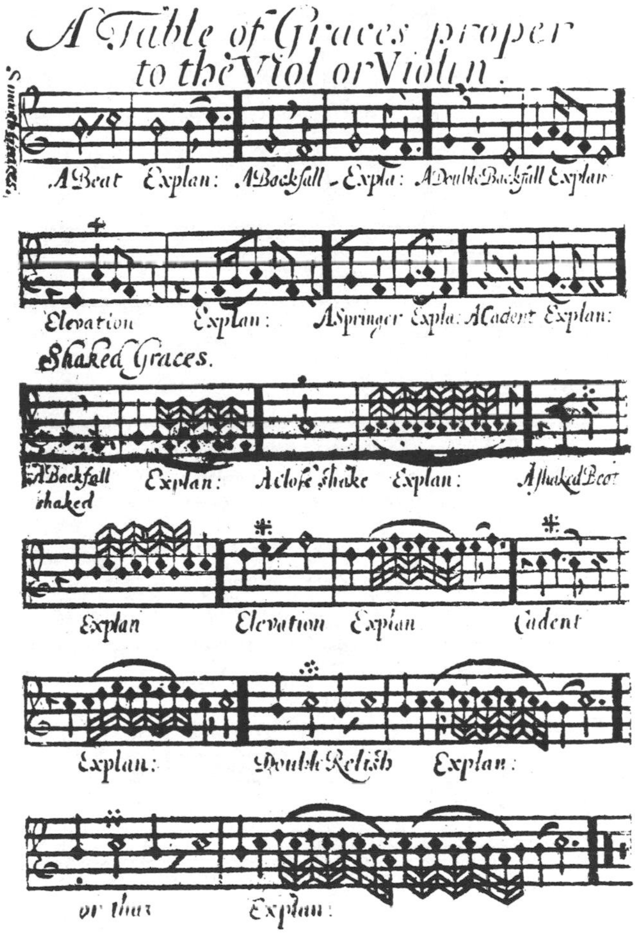
A Table of Graces proper to the Viol or Violin.
A Beat
Explan:
A Backfall
Expla:
A Double Backfall
Explan:
Elevation
Explan:
A Springer
Expla:
A Cadent
Explan:
Shaked Graces.
A Backfall shaked
Explan:
A close shake
Explan:
A shaked Beat
Explan
Elevation
Explan
Cadent
Explan:
Double Relish
Explan:
or thus
Explan:

Short

Short TUNES for the *TREBLE-VIOLIN* by Letters and Notes.

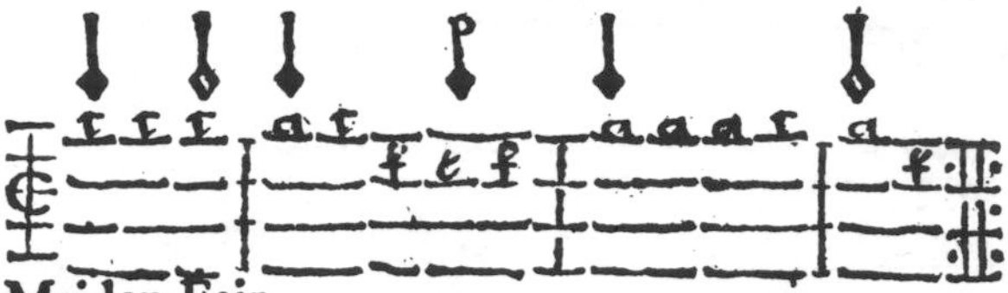

f f f a f f t f a a a f a f

Maiden Fair.

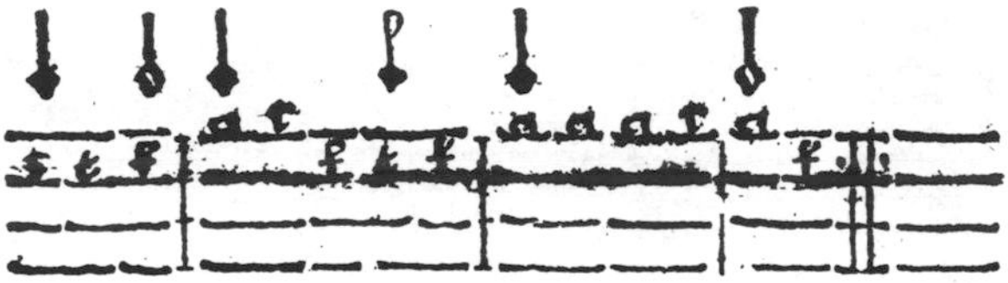

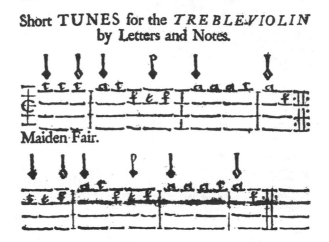

Note, *That in these Lessons by Letters the* Time *is not put over every Letter; but if a* Crotchet *be over any Letter, the following Letters are to be* Crotchets *also, till you see the Note changed; and the like is to be observed in other Notes.*

Maiden Fair.

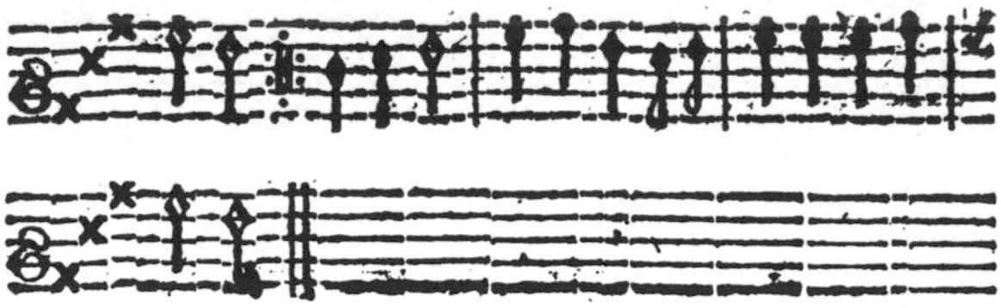

The

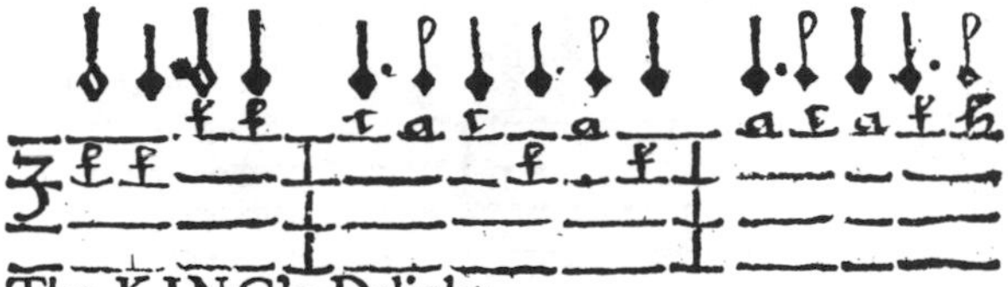

The KING's Delight.

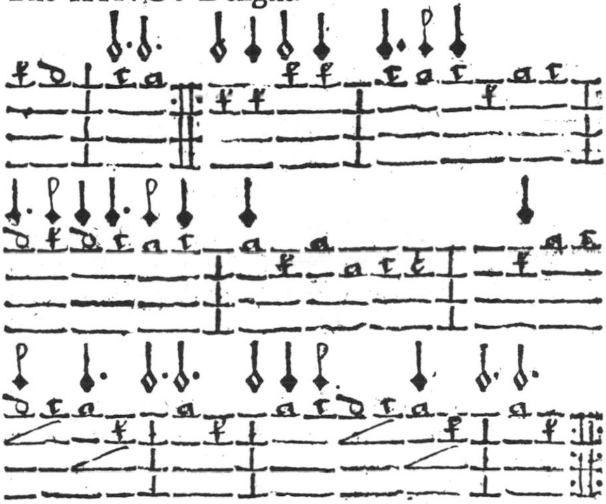

The KING's Delight.

Parthenia.

Parthenia.

John come kiss: With Division to each Strain.

The *Lark*, with Division.

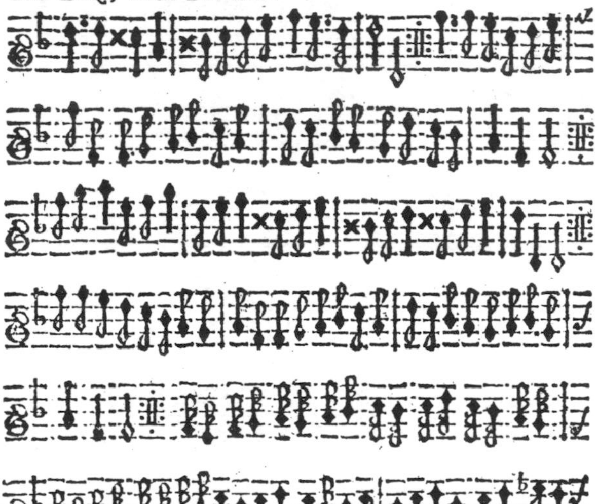

A BRIEF

A BRIEF INTRODUCTION To the ART of DESCANT: OR, Composing Musick in Parts.

The Third BOOK.

MUSICK is an Art of expressing perfect Harmony, either by *Voice* or *Instrument*; which Harmony ariseth from well-taken *Concords* and *Discords*.

In the *Scale* or *Gam-ut* there are seven Notes, *G, A, B, C, D, E, F*; for their Eighths are the same in nature of Sound. Of these seven, some are called *Cords* or *Concords*, and others *Discords*.

The *Concords* are four in number, *viz.* an *Unison*, a *Third*, a *Fifth*, and a *Sixth*.

The *Discords* are three in number, *viz.* a *Second*, a *Fourth*, and a *Seventh*.

The *Third*, *Fifth*, and *Sixth*, are either Perfect, or Imperfect. The Imperfect is less than the Perfect by half a Note: As,

A Third *Minor* includes four half Notes.
A Third *Major* includes five half Notes.
A Sixth *Minor* includes nine half Notes.
A Sixth *Major* includes ten half Notes.

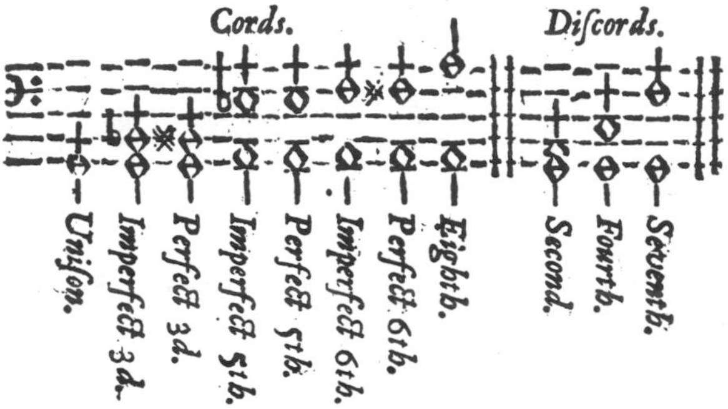
Cords.
Discords.
Unison.
Imperfect 3d.
Perfect 3d.
Imperfect 5th.
Perfect 5th.
Imperfect 6th.
Perfect 6th.
Eighth.
Second.
Fourth.
Seventh.

Example of the *Perfect* and *Imperfect Cords* and *Discords*, with their *Octaves*.

Perfect Cords.	*Discords.*	*Imperfect Cords.*	*Discords.*	*Perfect Cords.*	*Imperfect Cords.*	*Discords.*
1	2	3	4	5	6	7
8	9	10	11	12	13	14
15	16	17	18	19	20	21

With either of the *Perfect Cords* you may begin or end a Piece of MUSICK: The same with

with the *Third*, which is an *Imperfect*; but be ſure to avoid it with the *Sixth*.

In Compoſing of two or more Parts, the Parts do either ſtand ſtill; as,

Or the one doth ſtand ſtill, and the other move; as,

Or they both aſcend together; as,

Or both deſcend together; as,

Or the one doth aſcend, and the other deſcend; as,

The following RULES *will direct how the* Concords *are to be taken or applied every one of theſe ways.*

Rule I.

You may have as many *Thirds*, *Fifths*, *Sixths*, and *Eighths*, as you pleaſe ſtanding.

Rule II.

When one Part ſtandeth ſtill, and the other moves, the moving Part may move to any *Concords*; as,

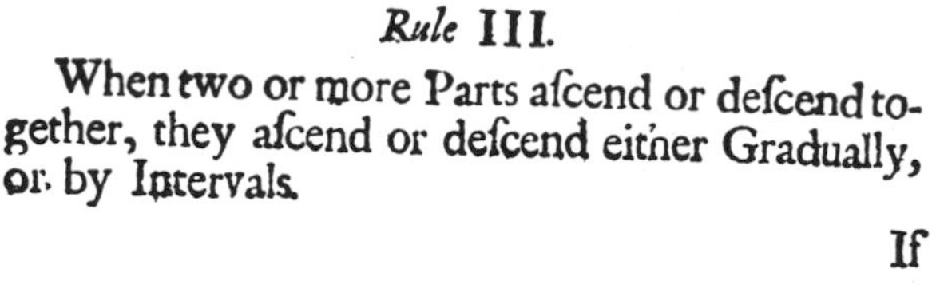

Rule III.

When two or more Parts aſcend or deſcend together, they aſcend or deſcend either Gradually, or by Intervals.

If

If they aſcend or deſcend Gradually, they do move by *Thirds:* You may have as many *Thirds* as you pleaſe; as,

Or aſcend or deſcend by *Sixths*; as,

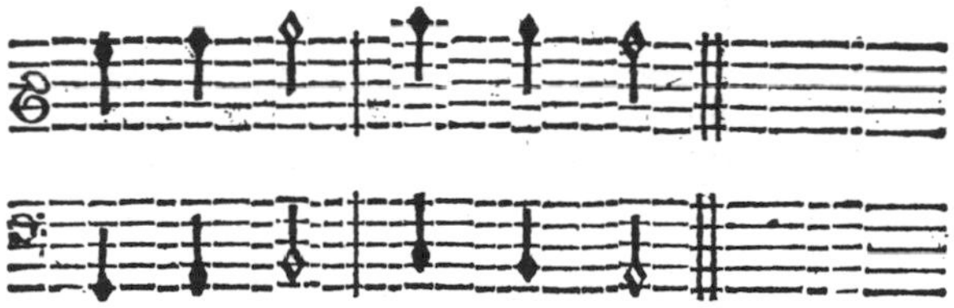

Take no more than two or three *Sixths:* Or they move by a *Fifth*, or a *Sixth*; as,

You may have as many *Notes* as you pleaſe.

If

If two Parts aſcend by Intervals, then you may move

From a	*Uniſon,*	to a	*Third*, or *Sixth.*
	Third,		*Third*, or *Sixth.*
	Fifth,		*Third*, or *Sixth.*
	Sixth,		*Third*, or *Sixth.*

Rule IV.

If two Parts do aſcend together Gradually, then as in the *Third Rule*: If by Intervals, you muſt move

From a	*Uniſon,*	to a	*Third*, or *Sixth.*
	Third,		*Third*, or *Fifth*, or *Sixth.*
	Fifth,		*Third*, or *Sixth.*
	Sixth,		*Third*, or *Sixth.*

Rule V.

If two Parts do move diverſly, as one aſcending, and the other deſcending; then thus,

Or upon the *Third*; Your *Baſs* muſt begin in the ſame Key, and end in the ſame Key.

An *Uniſon* is good, ſo it be in a *Minim* or *Crotchet*; but it is better if the one hold, and the other

other be going. Two *Eighths* aſcending or deſcending together is not lawful; nor two *Fifths*, unleſs one be the *Major*, and the other the *Minor Fifth.*

The uſe of Diſcords *on Holding-Notes.*

Rule I.

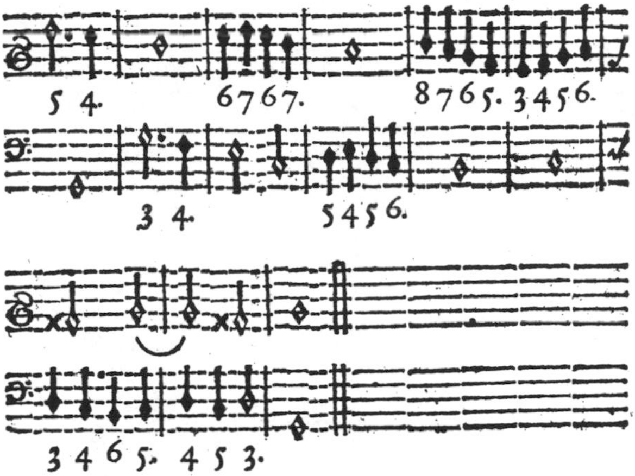
5 4. 6767. 8765. 3456.
3 4. 5456.
3 4 6 5. 4 5 3.

Rule II.

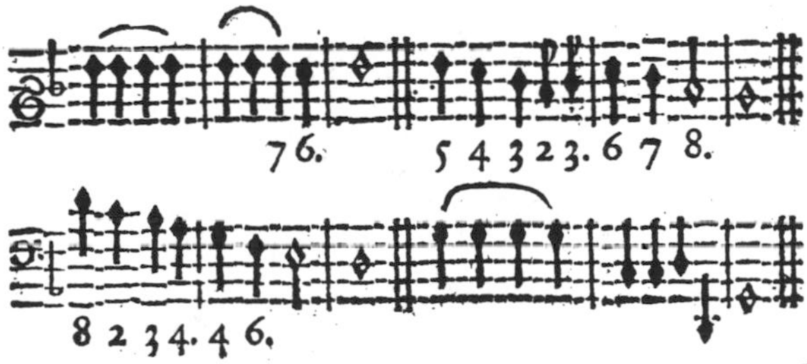
76. 5 4 323. 6 7 8.
8 2 34. 4 6.

Of

Of taking DISCORDS.

Discords are either taken by way of Paſs, or Binding.

Rule I.

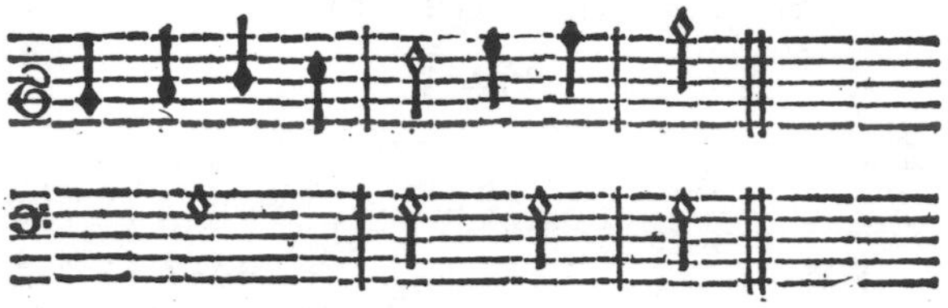

So thus you ſee, a *Diſcord* is placed between two *Concords*.

Rule II.

A *Diſcord* is bound three ſeveral ways; firſt, between the *Third*, and ſome other *Concord*: As,

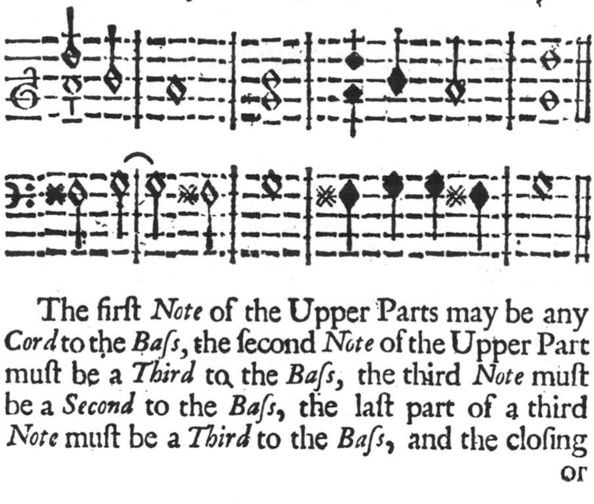

The firſt *Note* of the Upper Parts may be any *Cord* to the *Baſs*, the ſecond *Note* of the Upper Part muſt be a *Third* to the *Baſs*, the third *Note* muſt be a *Second* to the *Baſs*, the laſt part of a third *Note* muſt be a *Third* to the *Baſs*, and the cloſing

or fourth *Note* must be a *Third* or *Eighth* to the *Bass*, as in the foregoing Example.

The first *Note* of the *Bass* may be any *Concord* to the Upper Part, the first part of the second *Note* of the *Bass* must be a *Third* to the second *Note* of the *Treble* or Upper Part.

The last part of the second *Note* of the *Bass* must be a *Second* to the Upper Part, the third *Note* of the *Bass* must be a *Third* to the second part of the third *Note* of the *Treble*, and Close as in the aforesaid Example.

This Binding is seldom taken in a Close in more Parts than two; but in the middle of a Lesson it is to be taken as often as you shall see occasion. This Binding is seldom or never taken in other Notes than in this Example.

Rule III.

The third way of taking a *Discord* by way of Binding, is when the *Fourth* is taken between *Thirds*; as in the following Example.

So that you see the *Discords* are thus taken; *viz.* The first *Note* of the upper Part may be any *Note* to the

the *Bass*, the second *Note* of the upper Part must be a *Fourth* to the *Bass*, the eighth *Note* of the upper Part must be a *Third* to the *Bass*, and the Close must be an *Eighth* or a *Third*, as in the Example.

This Close may be used in any part of a *Lesson* of two or more Parts, either beginning, middle, or ending, but seldom to be omitted in the ending of a *Lesson*. This Close is seldom or never taken in longer or shorter *Notes* than in the Example.

Rule IV.

The fourth way of taking a *Discord* by way of Binding, is when the *Seventh* is taken between the *Sixth* and *Eighth*; as,

Rule V.

The fifth way of taking a *Discord* by way of Binding, is when the *Ninth* is taken between the *Third* and *Eighth*; as,

Several

Several Examples *of taking* Discords *elegantly.*

This Example shews the taking of Ninths *and* Sevenths *in two Parts.*

An Example of taking the Lesser Fourth.

An Example of taking the Greater Fourth.

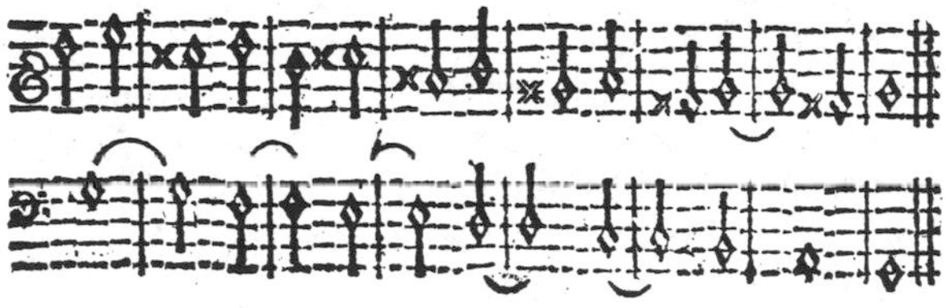

An

An Example of taking two Sevenths *in two Parts.*

7 7
7 7
7 7
7 7
7 7

In this *Example* you may obſerve the exact Method of taking two *Sevenths* together in whatſoever Key you ſhall Compoſe in, with this Allowance, That two *Major Sevenths* together is not good, but two *Minor Sevenths* together is allowable: Alſo if you take two *Sevenths*, ſo the one be *Minor* and the other *Major*, it is allowed, but be ſure the *Minor* be ſet before the *Major*, as you ſee in the Example.

Example

***Example of* Cadences *and* Bindings *in three Parts, with the* Cords *and* Discords *Figured as the Upper Parts stand to the* Bass.**

Rule I.
Rule II.
Rule III.
Rule IV.
A greater Third.
76
Rule V.
A lesser Third.
76

Observe, That when you make a Close, the *Bass* must always fall a *Fifth*, or rise a *Fourth*: And your upper Part must begin in the *Unison*, *Third*, or *Fifth*.

An Example of the usual Cadences *or* Closes *of two Parts.*

4 3.
4 3.
4. 3.
4 3.

RULES of Rising *and* Falling *one with another.*

It is not good to *rise* or *fall* with the *Bass* from a *Twelfth* or *Fifth* unto an *Eighth*, or from an *Eighth* unto a *Twelfth* or *Fifth*.

Example.

It

It is not good to *rise* with the *Bass* from a *Sixth* unto an *Eighth*, neither is it good to *fall* with the *Bass* from an *Eighth* unto a *Sixth*.

Example.

It is not good to *rise* from a *Fifth* to an *Eighth*, nor from an *Eighth* to a *Fifth*.

Example.

5 8. 8 5. 8 5.

Of the Passage of the Concords.

Two *Fifths* or two *Eighths* are not allowed together, either *rising* or *falling*, especially in two Parts.

(*Fifths not allowed.*)
(*Eighths not allowed.*)

(Fifths allowed.)
(Eighths allowed.)

The passing from a *Fifth* to an *Eighth*, or from an *Eighth* to a *Fifth*, may be allowable, so the upper Part remove but one degree of a Perfect Cord.

As for *Thirds* and *Sixths*, which are Imperfect Cords, *two*, *three*, or more of them ascending or descending together, are allowable.

It is good, and usual, to change from any one to any other different *Cord*, when any one of the Parts keeps its place; but two *Perfect Cords* ascending or descending is not allowed, unless it be in Composition of *Three*, *Four*, or *Five Parts*.

Example of Cords *not allowed in few Parts.*

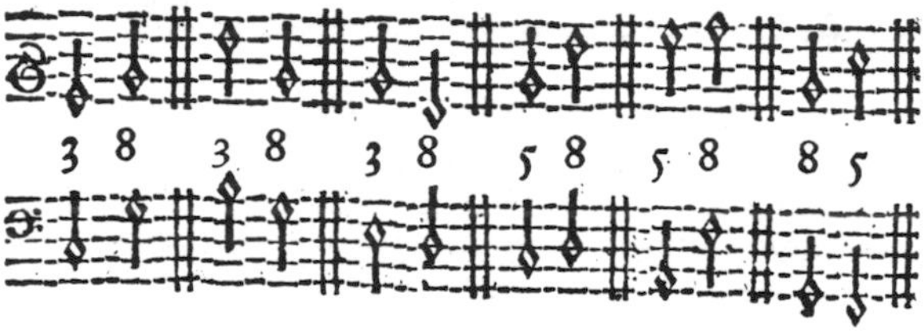
3 8 3 8 3 8 5 8 5 8 8 5

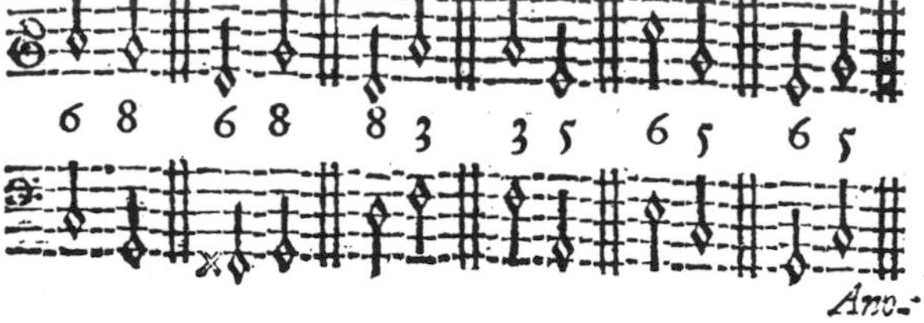
6 8 6 8 8 3 3 5 6 5 6 5

Ano-

Another Example.

(Good.)
(Not Good.)

In this Example, *F fa ut* Sharp in the *Bass* introduces *B fa b mi* Flat in the *Treble* very properly and well; but the next, where *F fa ut* is Flat in the *Bass*, and *B sharp* the following Note in the *Treble*, 'tis very Inharmonical, therefore to be avoided, for you will seldom meet with two full *Thirds* either ascending or descending, unless it be to prepare for a Close.

Note, That in few Parts *Imperfect Cords* are more pleasant and less cloying to the Ear than many *Perfect Cords*, especially in two Parts where *Eighths* and *Fifths* are least to be used, unless at the beginning or ending of a Piece of Composition, where Parts move contrary, one ascending, the other descending.

Formerly they used to Compose from the *Bass*, but Modern Authors Compose to the *Treble* when they make *Counterpoint* or *Basses* to Tunes or Songs.

As for Example.

8 6 3 3 5 3 3 5 8 5 3 5 8

Obſerve this always in Counterpoint, to avoid Tautology in ſetting a *Baſs* to a *Treble*, and let it be as Formal and Airy as the *Treble* will admit.

Let us a little examine this laſt Example. And now ſuppoſing there were no *Baſs* to the *Treble*, try Note by Note which is the propereſt *Cord* to each.

For the *Firſt Note*, you muſt certainly have an *Eighth*, becauſe it relates to the Key it is compoſed in.

For the *Second*, you have only two *Cords* to chuſe, *viz.* the *Sixth*, and *Third*; the *Fifth* you muſt not uſe, becauſe 'tis expected to the Note following to make a *Third*, therefore to be avoided, leſt you are guilty of that Tautology before-mentioned, and beſides there is not that Form and Variety which is required in few Parts; and an *Eighth* you cannot uſe neither, becauſe you run either into the Error of two *Eighths* together if you aſcend, or of cloying the Ear with too many *Perfect Cords* if you deſcend, therefore the *Third* or *Sixth* is the only Cords you can uſe; of theſe, the *Sixth* is much the beſt, for two Reaſons: Firſt, you move by contrary Motion to the *Baſs*, which is an Elegancy in two Parts; in the next place, you introduce the next Note more Harmonically with the *Sixth* than you can with the *Third*, but the *Sixth* muſt be *ſharp*, becauſe it has a nearer affinity to the Key.

The *Third Note* has a *Third*, which is generally the conſequence of a *Sixth*.

The

The *Fourth Note* cannot have a *Sixth*, becauſe of Tautology, it being the ſame as the *Third* before; the *Major Fifth* is not good, becauſe it has no relation to the Key; the *Minor Fifth* cannot do, by reaſon the following Note of the *Treble* does not move to the half Note below, which is the conſtant Rule of a falſe *Fifth* to introduce a *Third*; an *Eighth* is not ſo well, becauſe that is to be avoided as frequently as you can in two Parts, therefore the *Third* is the beſt Cord.

The *Fifth Note* cannot have an *Eighth*, becauſe 'tis the ſame Note as the former; a *Third* is not ſo well, by reaſon you do not obſerve the Rule of contrary Motions in aſcending when the other deſcends, and then you have had *Thirds* to the other two laſt Notes; therefore for variety a full Cord is beſt, and conſequently the *Fifth* to be preferred before the *Sixth*.

The *Sixth Note* cannot have an *Eighth*, becauſe 'tis the ſame Note as the former; a *Fifth* is not good; for fear of two *Fifths* together, a *Sixth* or *Third* are the only Cords, of which I eſteem the *Third* beſt, following the Rule of contrary Motions.

The *Seventh Note* cannot have an *Eighth*, by reaſon 'tis the ſame with the other; neither a *Fifth*, becauſe it makes no preparation for the next Note; therefore a *Sixth* or *Third* is the propereſt Cords, of which the *Third* in my opinion is beſt; for if you take the *Sixth*, it muſt be *ſharp*, and ſo make a *Third* to the following Note, which is what was done before in the first Bar, and for that reason to be omitted.

To the *Eighth Note* an *Eighth* cannot be made, because the same as before; a *Third* not so well, because you do not observe the Rule of contrary Motions; a *Sixth* not so good, because 'tis what must be used in the next Bar to make a Cadence, therefore the *Fifth* is best.

The *Ninth Note* cannot be a *Sixth* so properly, because 'tis the same with the former Note; a *Third* is not so well, by reason the fall or rising to it is Inharmonical; the *Fifth* is bad, having had a *Fifth* to the Note before, therefore the *Eighth* is the best Note.

The *Tenth Note* a *Sixth* must not be made too, it being the same as before; a *Third* not so well, because it must be *sharp*, and that is not gradual to rise too, and if you fall to it, you contradict the Rule of contrary Motions, though the Cord is good, yet I think not so formal as the other, which is the *Fifth*.

The *Eleventh Note* requires a *Third* more properly than any other Cord, for the *Sixth* would be the same with the foregoing Note and following, which must be to make a Close; the *Eighth* not so well, because so many Perfect Cords are not well, (as 'tis before observed;) a *Fifth* is Irregular, the Note before being a *Fifth*, which shews a *Third* is best.

The two last *Notes* is relating to the Cadence, therefore has a certain Rule.

Ha-

Having obſerved theſe *Rules* for making a Formal or Regular *Baſs* to a *Treble*, the next Thing to Treat of is the *Keys.*

There are but two *Keys* in Muſick, *viz.* a *Flat*, and a *Sharp*; not in relation to the Place where the firſt or laſt Note in a Piece of Muſick ſtands, but the *Thirds* above that Note. To diſtinguiſh your *Key* accordingly, you muſt examine whether the *Third* be *ſharp* or *flat*, therefore the firſt *Keys* for a Learner to Compoſe in ought to be the two Natural *Keys*, which are *A re* and *C fa ut*, the firſt the leſſer, the laſt the greater *Third*; from theſe all the other are formed, by adding either *Flats* or *Sharps.* When this is well digeſted, you muſt proceed to know what other Cloſes are proper to each *Key.*

To a *flat Key*, the Principal is the *Key* it ſelf, the next in dignity the *Fifth* above, and after that the *Third* and *Seventh* above.

Example.

Key.
5th.

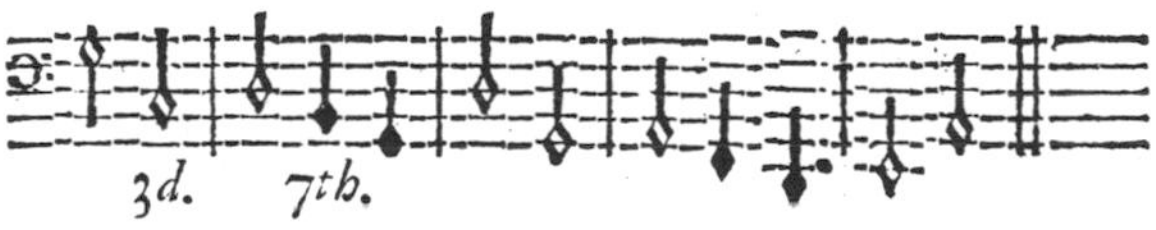
3d.
7th.

To a *ſharp Key*, the *Key* it ſelf firſt, the *Fifth* above, and in ſtead of the *Third* and *Seventh*, (which

(which are not ſo proper in a *ſharp Key)* the *Sixth* and *Second* above.

Example.

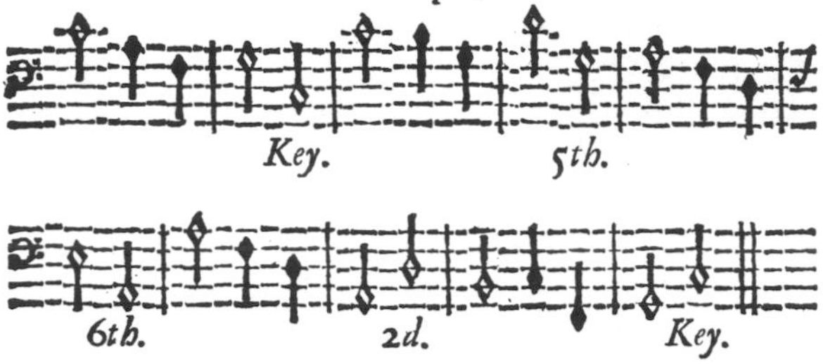
Key.
5th.
6th.
2d.
Key.

Theſe Examples are placed in the two open *Keys* to make it plainer, but tranſpoſe them into any other, they have the ſame effect; in applying of which Cloſes, you may uſe them promiſcuouſly as you pleaſe, only with this Caution, That you have regard to good Ayre.

There are ſome other Things to be obſerved in making a *Baſs* to a *Treble*, which ſhall be the next thing ſpoken of relating to *Fuge*.

Of Fuge, or Pointing.

A *Fuge*, is when one part leads one, two, three, four, or more Notes, and the other repeats the ſame in the *Uniſon*, or ſuch like in the *Octave*, a *Fourth* or *Fifth* above or below the Leading Part.

[☞ Under what Note you find this Mark /, the *Fuge* begins.]

Exam-

Example.

Fuge in the Fourth below.

Obſerve in this Example, that the *Treble* riſes a *Fifth*, and the *Baſs* but a *Fourth*, which is done becauſe it relates more to the Key than riſing a *Fifth*. So all *Fuges* in this nature are to be managed, if done Maſterly.

More to the ſame purpoſe.

The Treble riſes a 4th.
The Treble riſes a 5th.
The Baſs riſes a 5th.
The Baſs riſes a 4th.

There

There is another diminutive ſort of Fugeing called *Imitation* or *Reports*; which is, when you begin *Counterpoint*, and anſwer the *Treble* in ſome few Notes as you find occaſion when you ſet a *Baſs* to it.

As for Example.

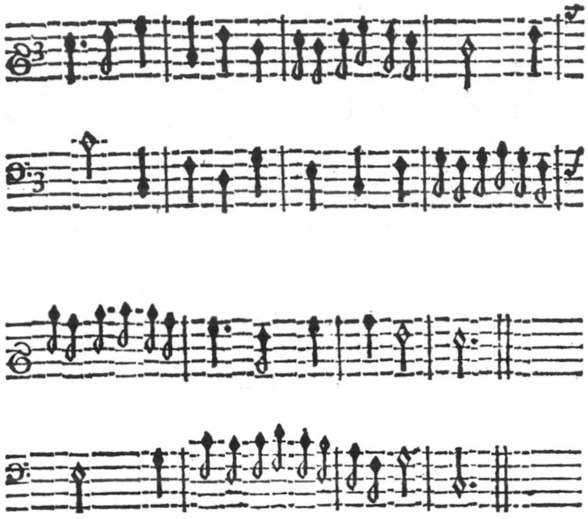

In the fourth, fifth, and ſixth Bar of the *Baſs*, it imitates the *Treble*.

The third ſort of Fugeing is called a *Double Fuge*; which is, when one Part leads a *Point*, and the following Part comes in with another, and ſo ſo the Parts change, as you may obſerve in the following Example, wherein I have made uſe of the former Point, and added another to it.

Example.

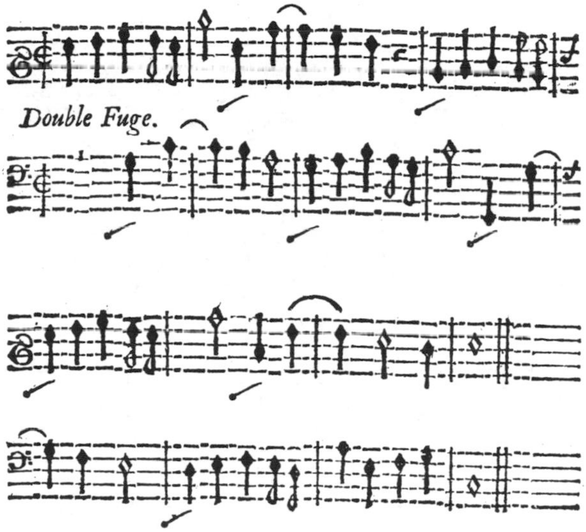
Double Fuge.

The fourth manner of Fugeing is called *Per Arſin & Theſin*, which admits of great Variety; and that is, when a Leading Part aſcends, the other deſcends exactly the ſame Notes. I have made uſe of the foregoing *Fuge*, that it may be more eaſie to a Learner.

As for Example.

Arsin.
Thesin.
Thesin.
Thesin.
Arsin.
Thesin.
Arsin.
Arsin.

A fifth sort of Fugeing is called *Per Augmentation*; that is, if the Leading Part be *Crotchets, Quavers*, or any other Notes in length, the following Part is augmented, and made as long again as the Leading Part. The following Example will explain it, which is contrived upon the same Fuge.

Exam-

Example.

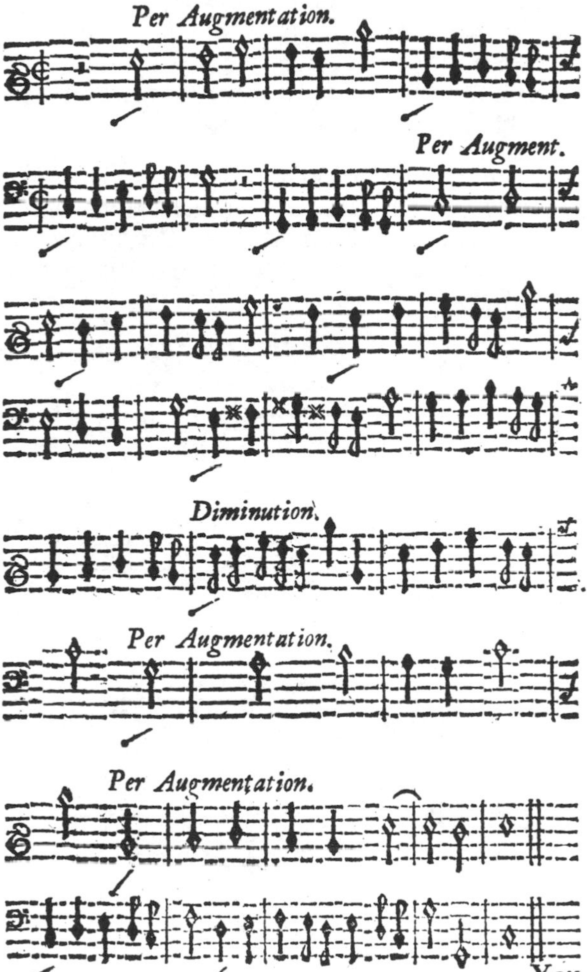
Per Augmentation.
Per Augment.
Diminution.
Per Augmentation.
Per Augmentation.

You

You may augment your Point to double or treble the length of your Leading Part, as you find occaſion; or diminiſh your *Fuge* for variety, as you may obſerve in the 10th Bar of the *Treble* in the Example foregoing.

This ſort of Fugeing is difficult, therefore ſeldom uſed unleſs it be in Canon.

There is a ſixth ſort of Fugeing called *Recte & Retro*, which is repeating the Notes backward; therefore you muſt avoid Prick'd Notes, becauſe in the Reverſe it would be of the wrong ſide of the Note.

Example upon the ſame Fuge.

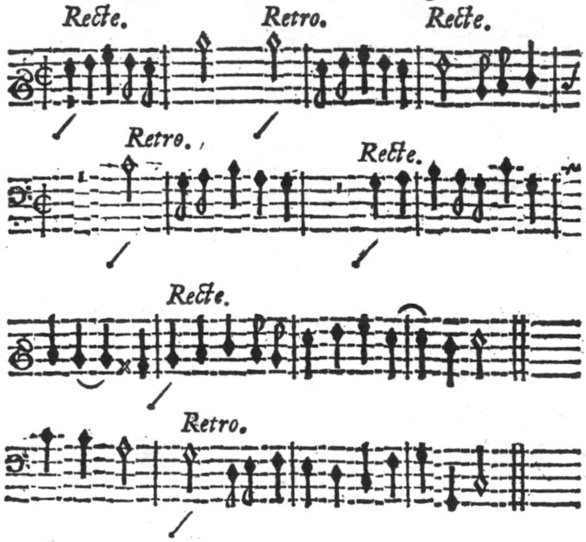
Recte.
Retro.
Recte.
Retro.
Recte.
Recte.
Retro.

This is a ſort of Muſick very rarely uſed, unleſs it be in Canon. There

There is a seventh sort of Fugeing called *Double Descant*, which is contrived so, that the Upper Part may be made the Under in the *Reply*; therefore you must avoid *Fifths*, because in the *Reply* they will become *Fourths*.

Example upon the same Fuge.

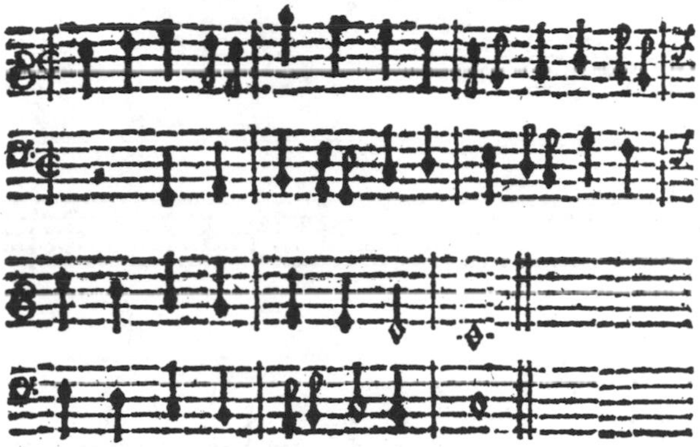

Reply.

The eighth and nobleſt ſort of Fugeing is *Canon*, the Method of which is to anſwer exactly Note for Note to the end.

Example upon the foregoing Fuge.

Canon in the 8th or 15th.

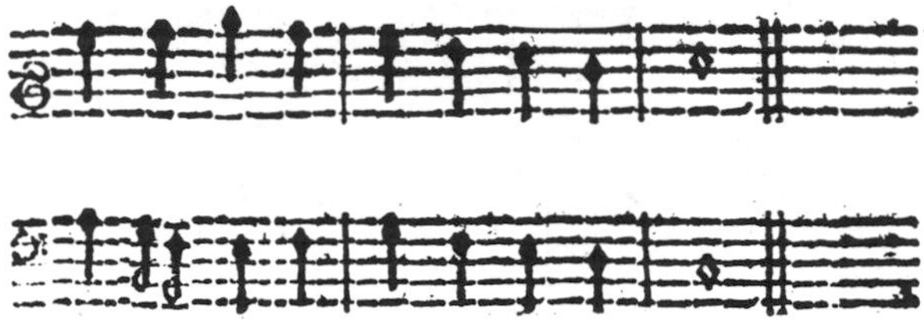

There is a wonderful variety of *Canons* in Mr. *Elway Bevin's* Book, Publiſhed in the Year 1631. to which I refer the Younger Practitioners, and ſo ſhall conclude with Two Parts, and go on to Three.

Composition of Three Parts.

THE first thing to Treat of is *Counterpoint*, and in this I must differ from Mr. *Simpson*, (whose *Compendium* I admire as the most Ingenious Book I e're met with upon this Subject;) but his Rule in Three Parts for *Counterpoint* is too strict and destructive to good Air, which ought to be preferred before such nice Rules.

His Example is this :

Treble.
Alt.
Bass.

Now in my opinion the *Alt* or *Second Part* should move gradually *Thirds* with the *Treble*; though the other be fuller, this is the smoothest, and carries more Air and Form in it, and I'm sure 'tis the constant Practise of the *Italians* in all their Musick, either Vocal or Instrumental, which I presume ought to be a Guide to us; the way I would have, is thus:

Example.

When you make a *Second Treble* to a Tune, keep it always below the Upper Part, becauſe it may not ſpoil the Air: But if you Compoſe *Sonata's*, there one *Treble* has as much Predominancy as the other; and you are not tied to ſuch a ſtrict Rule, but one may interfere with the other; as thus:

The ſame may be done in making Two Part *Anthems* to a *Thorow-Baſs*, or *Songs* that are Compoſed with deſign.

Fugeing in Three Parts is done by the ſame Rules as in Two, only you have more Scope and Variety. I ſhall make uſe of the ſame Point as I did in Two Parts, and give you ſome ſhort Examples in the ſeveral manners of *Fugeing*.

First Plain Fugeing.

The ſecond is *Imitation* or *Reports*, which needs no Example, becauſe you are confined to a *Treble*, aud ſo muſt make *Imitation* or *Reports* in the two Parts as the *Treble* will admit of.

The third is *Double Fugeing*, wherein I oblige my ſelf to the ſame Fuges as are uſed in the Two Parts.

Example.

When you make *Double Fuge* in Three Parts, you are not compelled to anſwer in the Third Part to the firſt Fuge any more than the ſecond, but are left to your pleaſure, as you ſee in the foregoing Example, where the *Baſs* anſwers to the firſt Fuge; you may as well anſwer the ſecond as firſt, according as you find it ſmootheſt to your Air, and moſt regular to your Deſign.

The fourth, *Per Arſis & Theſin* on the ſame Fuge.

Example.

Arsin.
Thesin.
Arsin.
Thesin.
Thesin.
Thesin.
Thesin.
Arsin.
Thesin.
Arsin.
Arsin.
Thesin.
Thesin.
Thesin.

The

The fifth, *Per Augmentation* on the same Fuge.

Example.

Per Augm.
Per Augm.
Per Augm.
Per Aug.
Per Augm.
Per Augm.

The

The ſixth, *Recte & Retro.*

Example.

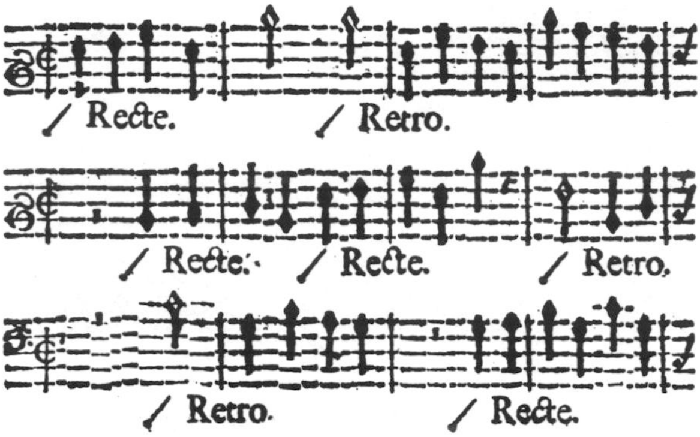
Recte.
Retro.
Recte.
Recte.
Retro.
Retro.
Recte.

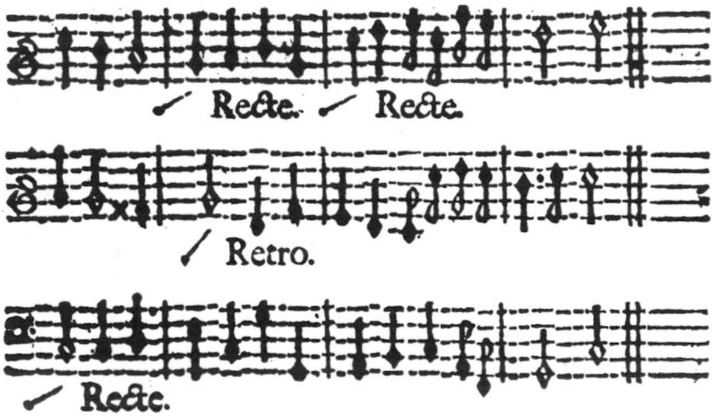
Recte.
Recte.
Retro.
Recte.

The ſeventh, *Double Deſcant*, in which I make but a ſhort Example, becauſe the two *Replies* ſhould not take up much room.

Exam-

Example.

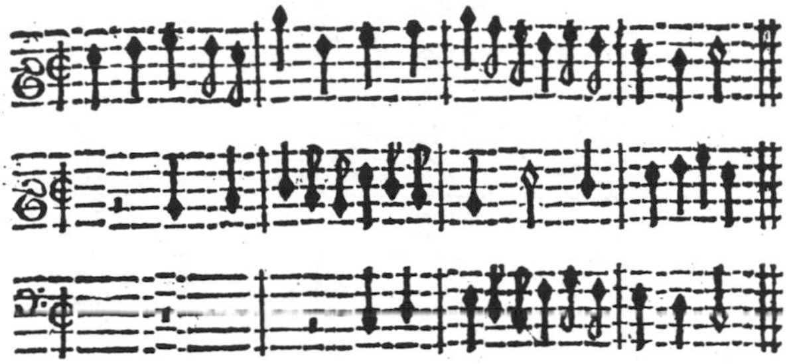

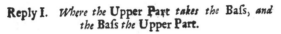

Reply I. *Where the* Upper Part *takes the* Bass, *and the* Bass *the* Upper Part.

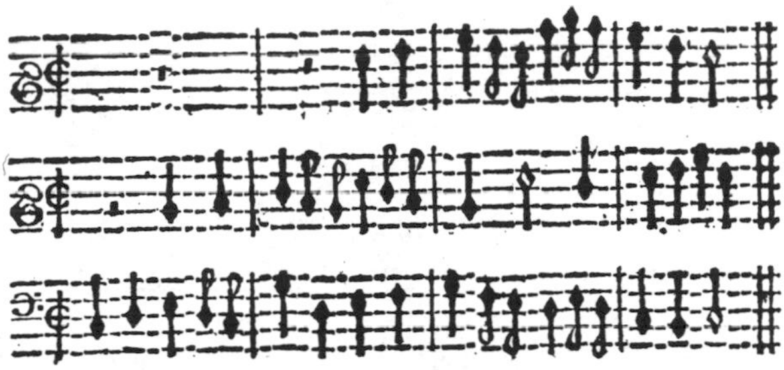

Reply II. *Where the* Second Treble *takes the* Bass, *and the* Bass *the* Second Treble.

Of

Of this ſort, there are ſome Fuges uſed by ſeveral Authors in *Sonata's*; a ſhort one I ſhall here inſert of the famous *Lelio Caliſta*, an *Italian*.

In

In making of ſuch-like you muſt avoid *Fifths*, as is before-mentioned in the *Rule* for Two Part *Double Deſcant*.

There is another ſort of *Fugeing* in three Parts before we come to *Canon*; which is, when each of them take a different *Fuge*, and ſo interchanges one with another like *Double Fugeing*.

As for Example.

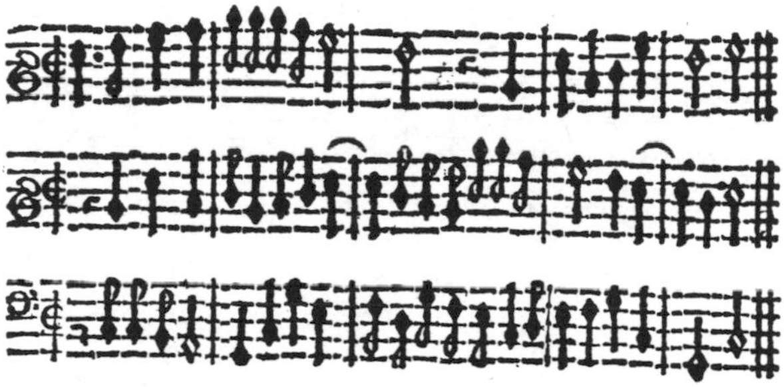

Moſt of theſe different ſorts of *Fugeing* are uſed in *Sonata's*, the chiefeſt Inſtrumental Muſick now in requeſt, where you will find *Double* and *Treble Fuges* alſo reverted and augmented in their *Canzona's*, with a great deal of Art mixed with good Air, which is the Perfection of a Maſter.

The next is *Canon*, of which I ſhall ſay but little, becauſe I refer you to the before-mentioned Book of Mr. *Bevin's*, where you will meet with all the Variety of *Canons* that are to be made, and ſhall only ſhew an Example of a *Gloria Patri* in Three Part *Canon*, ſo go on to four Parts.

A Ca-

A Canon, Three Parts in One.

Glo–ri–a
Glo––ri––a Pa—tri, & Fi–li-
Glo–ri–a Patri, & Fi——li——o, &

Pa—tri, & Fi—li—o, & Spi–ri–tu––i
o, & Spi–ri—tu––i Sancto, ſi–cut
Spi–ri–tù—i Sancto, ſi–cut e–rat in

San-cto, ſi—cut e-rat in prin-ci-pi-
e—rat in prin-ci-pi—o, & nunc, &
prin-ci-pi—o, & nunc, & nunc, & ſem-
o, & nunc, & nunc, & ſemper, & in
nunc, & ſemper, & in ſe—cu—la ſe-
per, & in ſe—cu—la ſe-cu—lo-rum;

ſe—cu—la ſe—cu-lo-rum; A———men, A-
cu-lo-rum; A ————men, Amen, A———
A————men, Amen, A—————

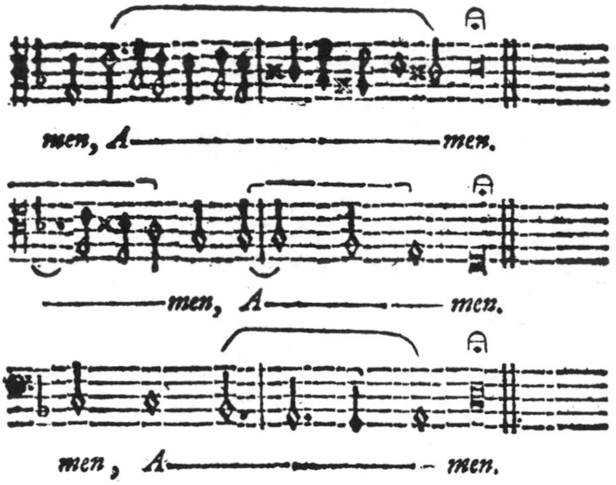
men, A————————————men.
————men, A—————men.
men, A———————————men.

Composition of Four Parts.

IN Church Musick, the four Parts consist generally of *Treble*, *Contra-Tenor*, *Tenor*, and *Bass*; in Instrumental Musick, commonly two *Trebles*, *Tenor*, and *Bass*: But always observe this Method, That in making four Parts Counterpoint, let your Cords joyn as near to the Upper Part as they can, for the Harmony is more agreeable to the Ear when the upper Parts are joyned close together, but still be sure to keep a smoothness and decorum, that none of the Inner Parts may make an Irregular Skip either upwards or downwards: If the *Treble* or Upper Part be a *Fifth* to the *Bass*, the other must be *Third* and *Eighth*; if the *Treble* be *Third*, the other must be *Eighth* and *Fifth*; so consequently, if the *Treble* be an *Eighth*, the other must be *Fifth* and *Third*.

Note: That in *C fa ut*, or any Key with a *sharp Third*, that to the half Note below the Key an *Eighth* is never made, nor to any accidental *Sharp* in a *flat* or *sharp* Key, either in the *Bass* or *Treble*, unless it be to introduce a Cadence. For Instance; If you make an *Eighth* to *B mi* in *C fa ut* Key, 'tis when the *Third* to *B mi* is *sharp*; and you design a Cadence in *E la mi*, otherwise 'tis never done, but the *Sixth* supplies the place of the *Eighth*, and commonly in four Parts a *Sixth* and false *Fifth* go together upon all *sharp* Notes.

As for Example.

Four Parts Counterpoint.

The falſe or defective *Fifth* is the only Note like a Diſcord that needs no preparation; and though it muſt not be uſed to begin a Piece of Mu-

Muſick with, yet there is no Cord whatſoever that has a more grateful Charm in it to pleaſe the Ear.

There are two *Diſcords* not yet Treated of in this ſhort *Introduction*, which I think proper now to mention, becauſe in an Example of four Parts you may ſee what other Cords belong to them, and that is, a *Sharp Seventh*, and *Flat Seventh*, two Notes mightily in uſe among the *Italian* Maſters; the *Sharp Seventh*, which generally reſolves it ſelf into the *Eighth*, you will find frequently in Recitative Songs, which is a kind of Speaking in Singing; a *Flat Seventh* reſolves it ſelf into a *Fifth*, and is uſed commonly at a Cloſe or Cadence. This Example will demonſtrate the thing plainer.

Example.

※7
4
2
b7
b5
3

Another Elegant Paſſage uſed by the ſame Authors.

The *Flat Sixth* before a Cloſe (as you may obſerve in the 2d *Treble*) is a Favourite Note with the *Italians*, for they generally make uſe of it.

There is another ſort of *Diſcord* uſed by the *Italians* not yet mentioned neither, which is the *Third* and *Fourth* together, to introduce a Cloſe.

As for Example.

In

In the ſame nature, if the *Baſs* ſhould continue in one place as the two *Trebles* do, you may move in the other Parts to what Notes you pleaſe, ſo you aſcend or deſcend gradually.

For Inſtance.

Theſe Inſtances were inſerted, to ſhew what Elegancies may be made in Counterpoint Muſick.

I ſhall proceed now to *Fuge* or *Pointing* in four Parts, in which I muſt follow the ſame Method as before, for there is no other ſort of Fugeing but what has been Treated of in three Parts, unleſs it be four *Fuges*, and that is made after the ſame manner as the three *Fuges*, of which there is an Example in Page 125.

First Plain Fugeing on the same Point.

The Second is *Imitation* or *Reports*, which needs no Example, for the aforesaid *Reasons* in three Parts.

The

The third is *Double Fugeing* on the ſame Fuges.

Example.

The fourth, *Per Arsin & Thesin.*

Example.

Arsin.
Thesin.
Arsin.
Thesin.
Thesin.
Arsin.
Thesin.

Thesin.
Arsin.
Thesin.
Arsin.

The

The Fifth, *Per Augmentation.*

Example.

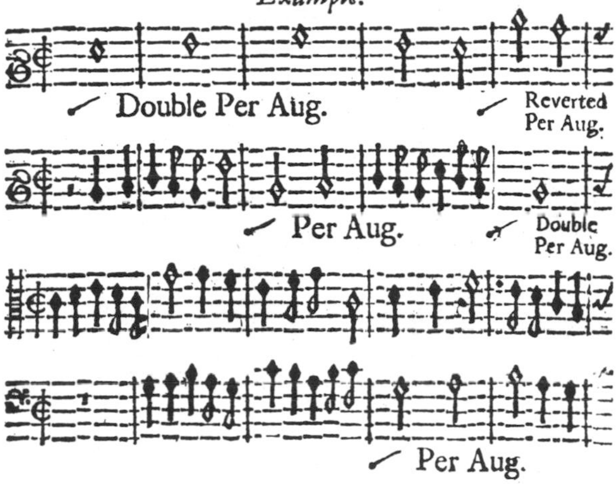
Double Per Aug.
Reverted Per Aug.
Per Aug.
Double Per Aug.
Per Aug.

Per Aug.
Revert. Per Aug.

The

The Sixth, *Recte & Retro.*

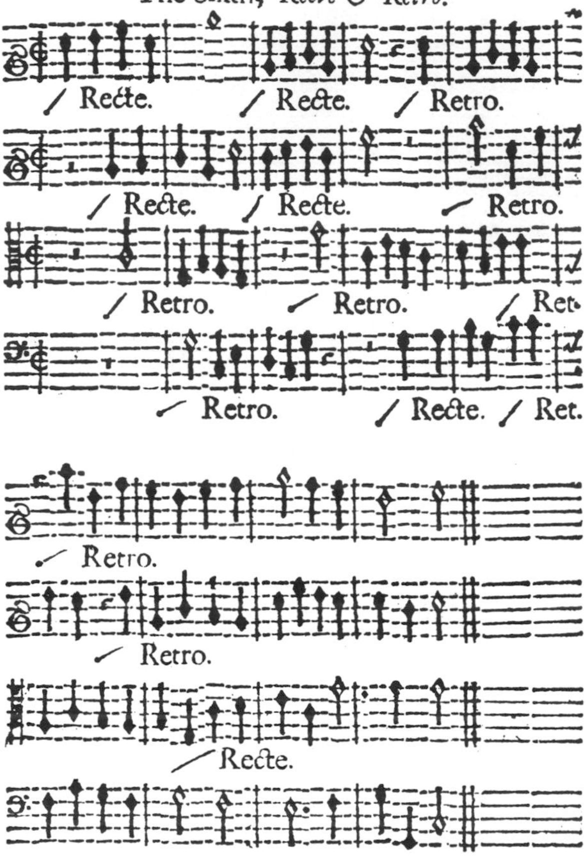
Recte.
Recte.
Retro.
Recte.
Recte.
Retro.
Retro.
Retro.
Ret.
Retro.
Recte.
Ret.
Retro.
Retro.
Recte.

The Seventh is *Double Descant*, which you hardly ever meet with in Four Parts, becauſe a *Fifth* muſt be avoided, therefore 'tis defective, and wants a Cord to fill up in ſo many Parts, for which Reaſon I ſhall omit an Example. The

The next is *Canon*, but before I Treat of that, there is one ſort of *Fugeing* to be mention'd, which is, Four Fuges carried on, interchanging one with another.

As for Example.

Canon in Four Parts is generally Four in Two, or Four in One: Here is an Example of each, which will ſhew the Method of making them.

A Canon; Four in Two.

Mi-ſe-re-re me-i, mi-ſe-re-re me—i, O Je-
Mi-ſe-re-re me-i, O Jeſu! O Je—ſu!
Mi-ſe-re-re me-i, mi-ſe-re-re me-
Mi—ſe—re-re me-i, O Je-ſu! O
ſu! O Jeſu! Mi—ſe—re—re me-i.
Mi-ſe-re-re mei Je—ſu! Mi-ſe-re-re me—i.
i, O Je—ſu! O Je—ſu me—i!
Je——ſu! Mi-ſe-re-re me-i Je——ſu!

This *Canon* of Four in One, is a *Gloria Patri* of Dr. *Blow's*, whose Character is sufficiently known by his Works, of which this very Instance is enough to recommend him for one of the Greatest Masters in the World.

A Canon, Four in One.

Glo–ry be to the Father, and to the Son,
Glo——ry be to the Father, and
Glo———-ry be to the
Glo—
and to the Ho——ly Ghost, the
to the Son, and to the
Father, and to the Son, and
—-ry be to the Fa–ther, and to the

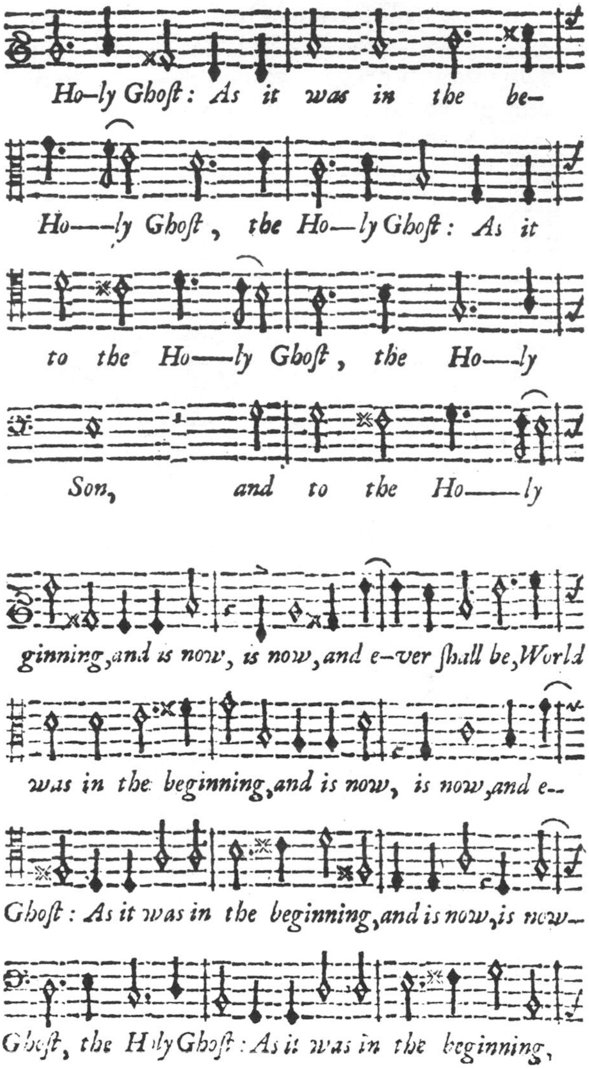
Ho-ly Ghoſt: As it was in the be-
Ho---ly Ghoſt, the Ho-ly Ghoſt: As it
to the Ho---ly Ghoſt, the Ho---ly
Son, and to the Ho---ly
ginning, and is now, is now, and e-ver ſhall be, World
was in the beginning, and is now, is now, and e--
Ghoſt: As it was in the beginning, and is now, is now--
Ghoſt, the Holy Ghoſt: As it was in the beginning,

without end. A———— men, A——
—ver shall be, World without end. A————
—, and ever shall be, World without end. A———
and is now, is now, and ever shall be, World without
————men.
men, A————men.
——men, A————men.
end. A————men.

Compo-

Composition of Five or more Parts,

IS ſtill by adding another *Octave* or *Uniſon*, for there is but Three Concords, *viz. Third, Fifth*, and *Eighth*, therefore when you make more than Three Parts in Counterpoint, 'tis by repeating ſome of the ſame Cords over again.

One Thing that was forgot to be ſpoken of in its proper place, I think neceſſary to ſay a little of now, which is Compoſing upon a *Ground*, a very eaſie thing to do, and requires but little Judgment: As 'tis generally uſed in *Chacones*, where they regard only good Air in the *Treble*, and often the *Ground* is four Notes gradually deſcending, but to maintain *Fuges* upon it would be difficult, being confined like a *Canon* to a *Plain Song*. There are alſo pretty *Dividing Grounds*, of whom the *Italians* were the firſt Inventors, to Single *Songs*, or *Songs* of Two Parts, which to do neatly, requires conſiderable Pains, and the beſt way to be acquainted with 'em, is to ſcore much, and chuſe the beſt Authors.

As for *Fugeing*, 'tis done by the ſame Methods as has been before obſerved.

All that I ſhall further add, is to wiſh, That what is here mentioned may be as Uſeful as 'tis Intended, and then 'twill more than Recompence the Trouble of the Author.

F I N I S.

Appendix I

"Of the Several Keys in Musick . . . ," Chapter VII and "Of the Trill, or Shake," Chapter VIII from the Thirteenth Edition

CHAP. VII.

Of the ſeveral KEYS *in* Muſick; *alſo what a* Key *is, and how to Name your* Notes *in any of them.*

HAving already given you ſome Hints of the *Flats* and *Sharps*, I ſhall now proceed to Inſtruct you in the further Uſe of them, with the ſeveral Alterations of *Keys* they produce by being plac'd at the beginning of the five Lines; but before I proceed any farther, I think it requiſite to let you know what a *Key* is. For Inſtance; Suppoſe you have a Leſſon or Song prick'd down, you muſt obſerve in what Space or Line the laſt Note of it ſtands on, and that is the *Key:* Now it very often begins in the *Key*, but ſometimes a *Third* or *Fifth* above it, and ſo you cannot ſo well tell, but it certainly ends in it.

A *Key* is a Song or Tune depending on a Sound given, as a Sermon does on a Text, and when it ends right, it gives ſuch a Satisfaction to the Ear, that nothing more is expected after it; like a Period at the end of a Sentence, when the Senſe is full, and no more depending upon it.

You muſt always Name your *Keys* in reference to the *Baſs.*

As for Example.

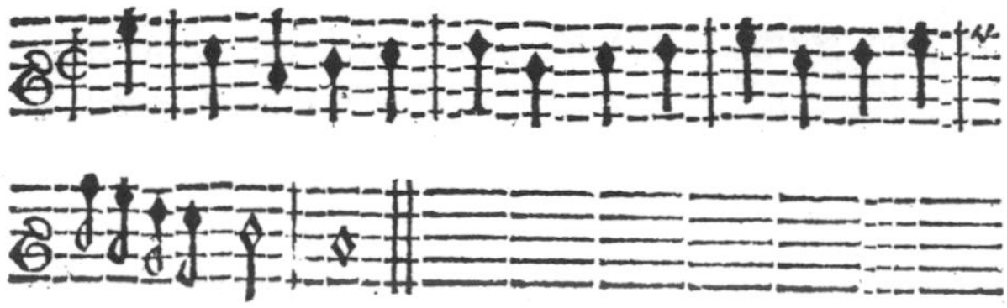

This Leſſon is ſet in *Are* Key, thô you ſee it begins in *Ela*, a Fifth above it.

Now ſuppoſe you were ask'd what *Key* this Leſſon is in, you muſt not ſay *Alamire* becauſe it ends there, but *Are*, in reference to the *Baſs*, as I ſaid before.

There are but two *Keys* in Muſick, one *flat*, and the other *ſharp*, which is ſufficient to write down any *melancholy* or *chearful Song* whatever. The *melancholy* or *flat* Key, without either *flat* or *ſharp* at the beginning, is *Are* or *Alamire*; the *ſharp* or *chearful Key*, without *flat* or *ſharp* at the beginning, is *C faut* or *C ſolfa*: Theſe we call the two *Natural Keys*, becauſe a Song may be ſet in either of them without the help of *Flats* or *Sharps*; which cannot be done in any other *Key*, but there muſt be either *Flats* or *Sharps* placed at the beginning of your five Rules or Lines.

The principal *Keys* made uſe of, are as follow: *Gamut* Flat and Sharp, *Are* Natural and Sharp, *B mi* Natural and Flat, *C faut* Natural and Flat, *D ſolre* Natural and Sharp, *Elami* Natural

tural and Flat, and ſometimes Sharp; *F fa ut* Natural and Flat, and ſometimes Sharp. There may be more thought on to puzzle Young Beginners, but not of any Uſe, here being Variety enough to pleaſe the Ear.

Now you'l never meet with any Song or Tune, but 'tis ſet in one of theſe *Keys* I juſt now mention'd; I would therefore adviſe you to Sing or *Solfa* well in the two *Natural Keys* before you proceed to the reſt, and then you'l acquire the Knowledge of them with much greater eaſe.

I ſhall now proceed to ſet this *flat* Leſſon, which is in *Are*, in all the reſt of the *flat* or *melancholy Keys*, and ſhall begin with *Gamut*.

Example.

Gamut Flat.

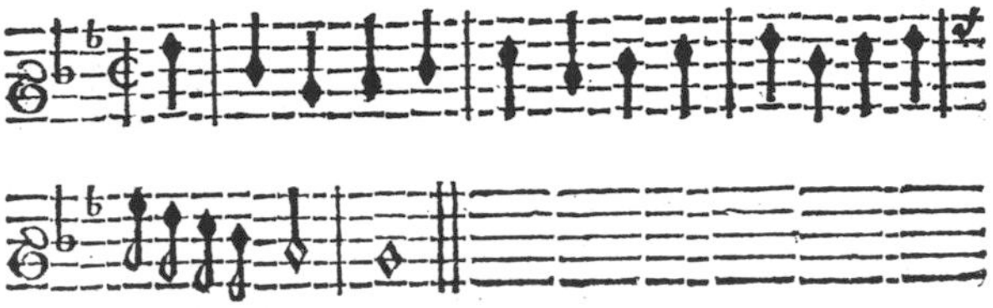

Are, the Natural Key.

B mi

B mi Natural.

C *faut* Flat.

D solre Natural.

Elami Natural.

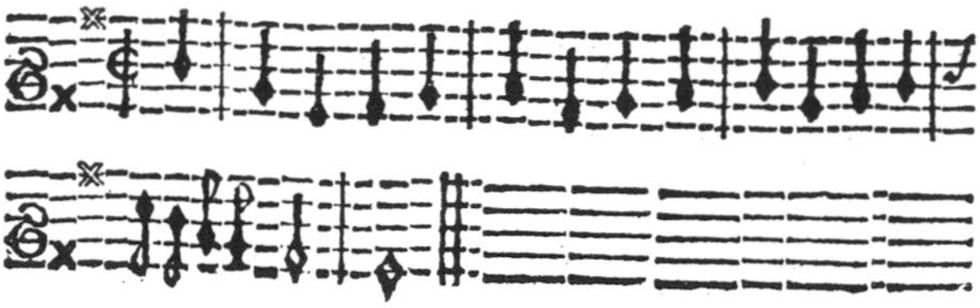

F faut

F faut Flat.

F faut Sharp.

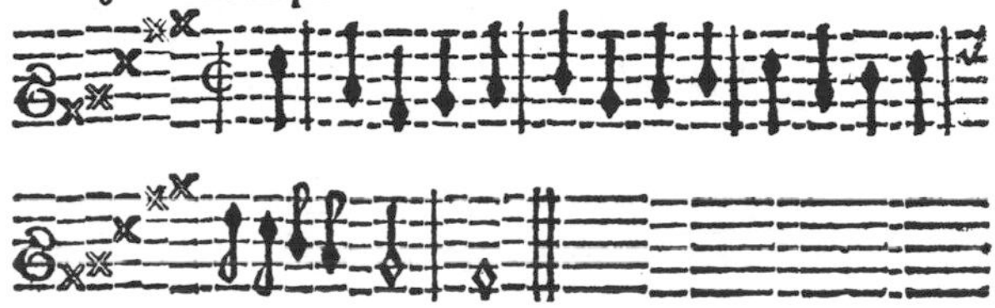

Get but a *Violin* to play this Leſſon over, and you'l find the ſame Air through all, as in your *natural Key*; ſo that the difficulty of *Solfaing* in any of theſe *melancholy* or *flat Keys*, is to apply them all to *Are* Key, and then you cannot fail.

For Example: The firſt *Note* of your Leſſon in the *natural Key* you call *La*, which ſtands in the uppermoſt Space of the five Lines; now in the reſt of the *Keys* you may obſerve the firſt *Note* to be in a different Place according to the difference of the *Keys*; but you ought to give every *Note* the ſame Name in theſe Seven ſeveral *Keys* as you do in the *natural Keys*, for the Reaſon I gave you before, reconciling all *melancholy Keys* to *Are Key*, and all *chearful Keys* to *C faut Key*. Alſo abſerve well the Number of the *Flats* or *Sharps* that occaſion the ſeveral Variations.

I

I ſhall now proceed to a Leſſon in your *Natural Sharp* or *Chearful Key*, which is *C faut*, and ſo go through the reſt of the *chearful Keys*, as I have done the *flat* Ones.

For Example.

Gamut Sharp.

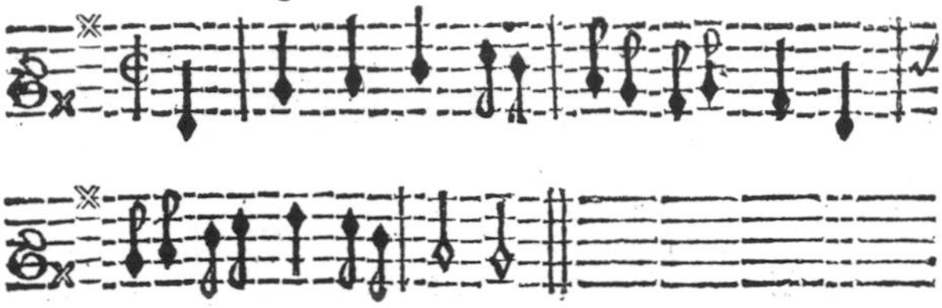

Are Sharp.

B mi Flat.

C *faut*,

C faut, the Natural Key.

D solre Sharp.

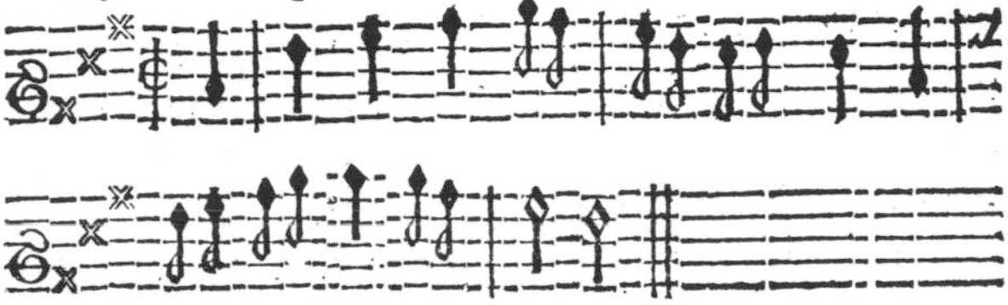

Elami with Flats.

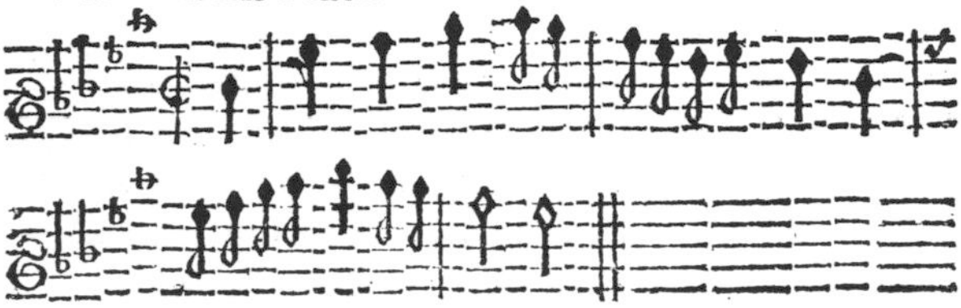

Elami with Sharps.

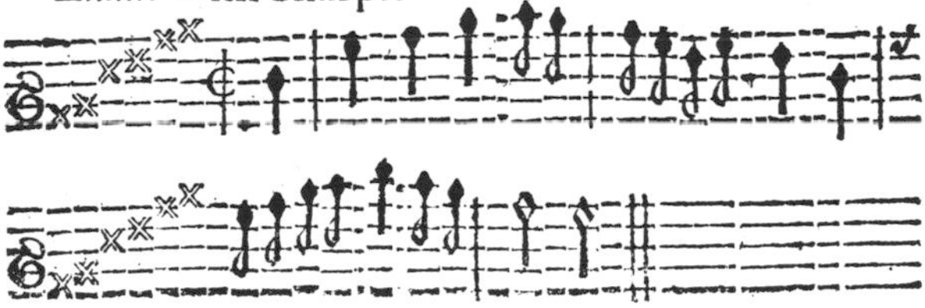

F faut.

F faut.

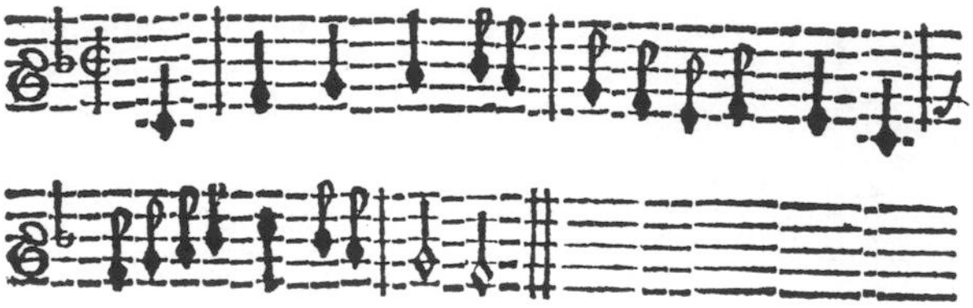

The ſureſt way to underſtand theſe ſeveral *Keys*, is firſt to get Leſſons in the two *natural* Ones till you are perfect in them, and then proceed to one *Flat*, and ſo on to two or more till you have conquer'd all. The like Method you muſt obſerve with the *Sharps*.

I would adviſe you at the firſt to get any *Song* you meet with put into one of the *natural Keys*; alſo I would have you make uſe of the *Treble Cliff*, being always plac'd on the ſecond Line from the bottom of your five; the *Baß Cliff* is not ſo common as that, althô it's as certain as the other; but the *Tenor Cliff* is very uncertain, for you may find it plac'd on every Line of the five except the uppermoſt, obſerving that whatever Line it ſtands on you ought to call it *C ſolfaut*, as if it ſtood upon the middle Line, and the *Notes* below and above it equally the ſame, as in the *Scale* or *Gamut*.

Let me entreat you to Practice your Leſſons for a conſiderable time prick'd down in theſe two *Keys*, *Are*, and *C faut*, before you proceed to the other; and believe, that nothing but a diligent Application will overcome the Difficulties you'l meet with in this Science.

CHAP.

CHAP. VIII.

Of the TRILL, *or* SHAKE.

THE *Trill* is the most principal Grace in Musick, and the most used; the Directions for Learning it is only this, To move your Voice easily upon one Syllable the distance of a Note, thus:

Mi la, mi la,
sol sol.

First move *slow*, then *faster* by degrees, and you'l find it come to you with little Practice; but beware of huddling your Voice too fast, for *B fabemi* and *Alamire* ought both of them to be sounded distinctly, your *Shake* being compounded either of a whole or half Tone. This is the Method, which observ'd with a diligent Practice, will certainly gain your Ends.

I shall add a few *Instructions* to let you know where the *Trill* ought to be used: *(Viz.)* On all Descending *Prick'd Crotchets*, also when the *Note* before is in the same Line or Space with it, and generally before a *Close*, either in the middle, or at the end of a Song. I wil now set you a small Example of it, and place a *Cross* over the Notes you ought to *shake*.

Exam-

Example.

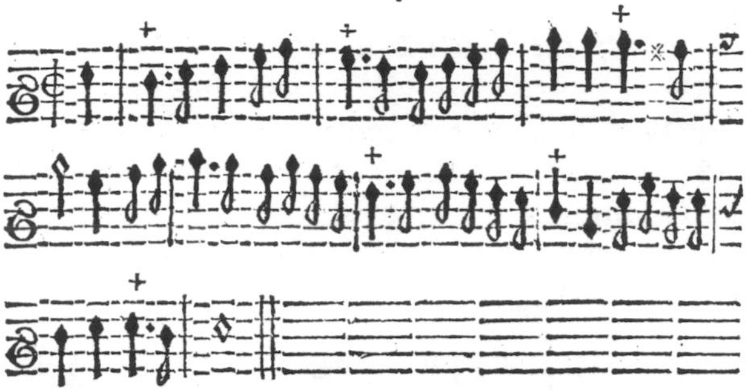

There are other *Notes* which ought to be *ſhak'd* beſides *Prick'd Notes*, and a little Practice upon theſe Directions will be much more Advantageous than what I can ſay here.

I hope I have laid before you, by plain and familiar Examples, the Theory or Ground of *Plain Song*, which (if well digeſted) will be a ſufficient Foundation for an Improvement of your Knowledge. Alſo I would have you hear as much *Muſick* perform'd as you can, which will be very beneficial to you. All that I can ſay more, is to fling in my beſt Wiſhes to your Endeavours, and ſo I bid you heartily

Farewel.

SOME

Appendix II

"Short Ayres or Songs of Two Voices, Treble and Bass, for Beginners" from the Fourteenth Edition

Short AYRES *or* SONGS *of Two Voices,* Treble *and* Bass, *for Beginners.*

A 2 Voc. *TREBLE.* *W. L.*

G-Ather your Rose-buds while you may, old
Time is still a fly--ing, and that same Flow'r that
smiles to day, to mor—row will be dy—ing.

A 2 Voc. BASS. *W. L.*

G-A—ther your Rose-buds while you may, old
Time is still a fly---ing, and that same Flow'r that
smiles to day, to morrow will be dy—ing.

A 2 Voc. *TREBLE.* *J. P.*

Omely Swain, why sits thou so? *Fa la la la la*
la la la. Fold-ed Arms are signs of wo,
Fa la la la la la la la la la.

If thy Nymph no favour show,
Fa la la, &c.
Chuſe another let het go,
Fa la la, &c.

Fa la la la la la la la la la la.
la la la. Fold-ed Arms are ſigns of wo,
Omely Swain, why ſits the ſo? *Fa la la la la la la*

A 2 Voc. *BASS.* *J. P.*

A 2 *Voc.* TREBLE. *B. R.*

I
N the merry month of *May*, in a morn by break of day,
forth I walkt the wood so wide, when as *May* was in her pride,
there I spi-ed all a-lone, *Phi-li-da* and *Co--ri-don.*

there I spied all a-lone *Phi-li--da* and *Co--ri-don.*
forth I walkt the wood so wide, when as *May* was in her pride,
I
N the merry month of *May*, in a morn by break of day,

A 2 *Voc.* BASS. *B. R.*

A 2 Voc: TREBLE. T. B.

T
Urn *Amaril--lis* to thy Swain, turn *Amaril--lis*
to thy Swain, turn *Amaril--lis* to thy Swain, thy
Damon calls thee back again, thy *Damon* calls thee back a—
—gain: Here is a pretty, pretty, pretty, pretty, pretty
Arbor by, where *Apollo*, where *Apollo*, where *Apollo*,
where *A-pollo* cannot, cannont ſpy, where *A—pollo*
cannot ſpy. Here let's ſit and whilſt I play

Turn over

D 3

A 2 Voc. *BASS.* *T. B.*

Urn *A-ma-ril-lis* to thy Swain, turn *Amarillis*,
turn *A-ma—ril-lis*, turn *A-ma-ril-lis* to thy Swain,
thy *Damon* calls the back a—gain, thy *Da--mon*
calls thee back a—gain , Here is a pret--ty
Arbor by, where *A—pol--lo*, where *A—pollo*,
where *A--pollo*, where *A—pol--lo*, cannot ſpy, where *A—*
—-pollo, cannot ſpy: There let's ſit and whilſt I play,

TREBLE.

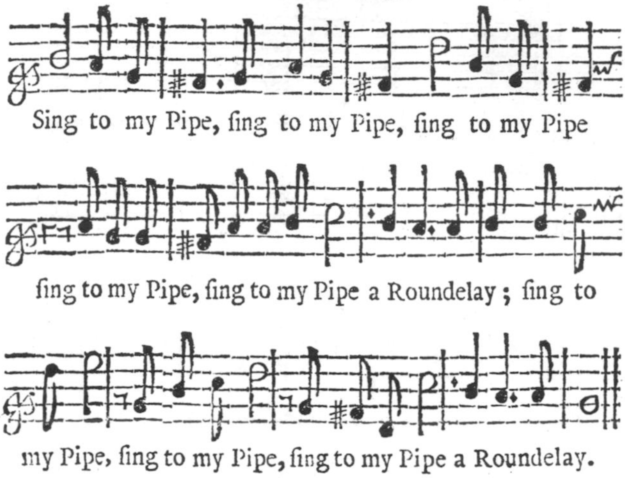
Sing to my Pipe, sing to my Pipe, sing to my Pipe
sing to my Pipe, sing to my Pipe a Roundelay; sing to
my Pipe, sing to my Pipe, sing to my Pipe a Roundelay.

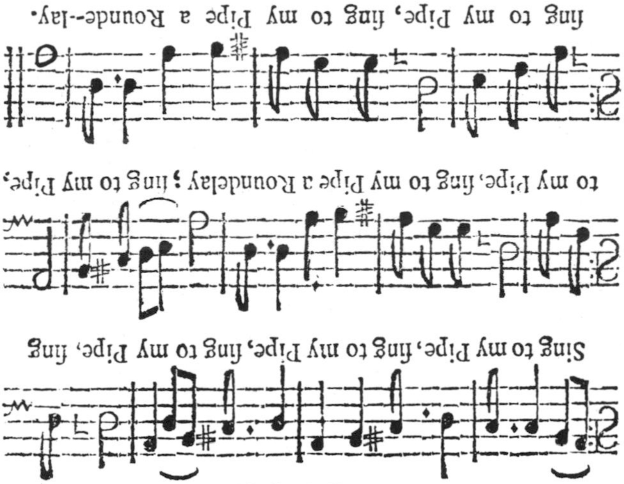
Sing to my Pipe, sing to my Pipe, sing to my Pipe, sing
to my Pipe, sing to my Pipe a Roundelay; sing to my Pipe,
sing to my Pipe, sing to my Pipe a Rounde--lay.

BASS.

A 2 Voc. TREBLE. *J. G.*

WIll *Cloris* cast her Sun-bright Eye upon so
mean a Swain as I? Can she af--fect my oaten Read?
or stoop to wear my Shepherds weed.

What rural sport can I devise,
To please her Ears, to please her Eyes?
Fair *Cloris* sees, Fair *Cloris* hears,
With Angels Eyes, and Angels Ears.

A 2 Voc. BASS. *J. G.*
WIll *Cloris* cast her Sun-bright Eye upon so
mean a Swain as I? Can, she affect my oaten Read?
or stoop to wear my Shepherds weed.

A 2 Voc. TREBLE. H. L.

Ome *Cloris* hye we to the Bow'r, to ſport us e're
the day be done; ſuch is thy pow'r, that ev'ry Flow'r
will ope to thee as to the Sun.

The wanton Suckling and the Vine
Will ſtrive for th' honour, who firſt may,
With their green Arms incircle thine,
To keep the burning Sun away.

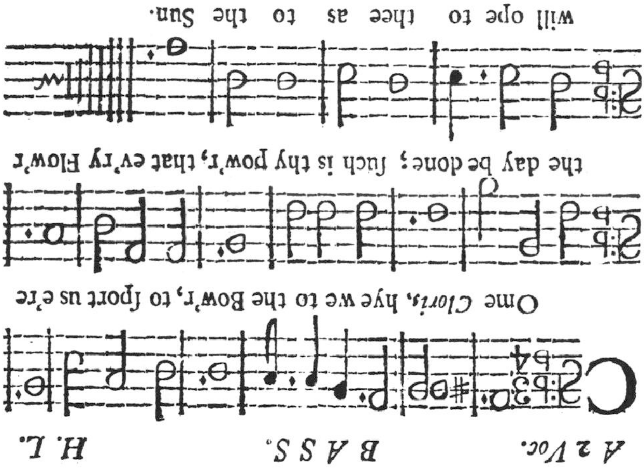
Ome *Cloris*, hye we to the Bow'r, to ſport us e're
the day be done; ſuch is thy pow'r, that ev'ry Flow'r
will ope to thee as to the Sun.

A 2 Voc. BASS. H. L.

Appendix III

"Some Tunes of the Most Usual Psalms, Broken for the Violin" from the Fourteenth Edition

Some TUNES *of the most usual* PSALMS, *Broken for the* VIOLIN.

Canterbury. *Psalm 23. and to all of 8, and 6.*

Martyrs. *Psalm 34, and to all of 8, and 6, Sillables.*

St. Davids. *Psalm 95, and to all of 8, and 6.*

Psalm 148.

St. Mary's. *Psalm.* 91, *and to all of* 8 *and* 6.

York. *Psalm* 78, *and to all of* 8, *and* 6.

Psalm 100.

Windser Tune. *Psalm,* 17, *and to all of* 8, *and* 6.

The End of the Second Book.

Appendix IV

"Canon Three in One" and "Canon in the Unison" from the Fourteenth Edition

Canon Three in One.

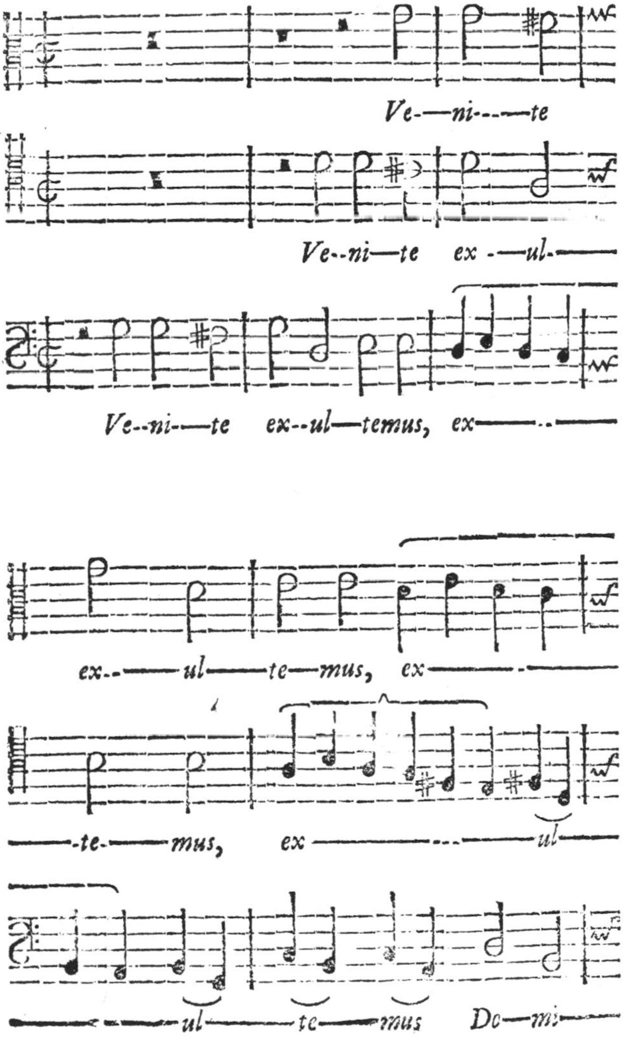
Ve-—ni-——te
Ve--ni—te ex -—ul-——
Ve--ni-—te ex--ul—temus, ex——
ex--——ul——te—mus, ex——
——-te-——mus, ex ———ul——
——ul——te——mus Do—mi——

——ul——te—mus Do—mi—no,
——te——mus Do—mi——no, Ju——
——no, Ju——bi—lemus De—o

Ju—bi——le—mus De—o ſa—lu——
——bi—le-mus De—o, ſa—lu—ta—ri
ſa——lu—ta—ri No—ſtro.

Beg in again.
—-ta- ri No—ſtro. Venite,
Begin again.
No-—ſtro. Ve --ni--te,
Begin again.
Ve--ni--te,

Ca-

Canon in the Unison.

Lauda-te De--um om-nes gen-tes,
om--nes gen——tes, Laudate De—um
om--nes gen—tis, Lau-da-te eum Lau—
——-da——te, Lau-—-da——te, Lau——
——da———te, Laudate e--um omnis
po—pu-—-li.

Appendix V

Facsimiles of Portraits of John Playford from the 1660, 1662, 1664, and 1670 Editions

Cantate Domino Canticum nov:
Ætat. Suæ 38
Non Nobis Domine
R Gaywood fecit

This, PLAYFORD's Shadow doth present;
Peruse his Booke and there you'le see
His whole Designe is Publique Good
His Soule and Minde an Harmonie.

D. Loggan sculp.
IOHANNIS
PLAYFORD

Cantate Domino Canticum nov:
Ætatis Suæ 40
Ano. Dom: 1663
Non Nobis Domine

This, PLAYFORD's Shadow doth present;
Peruse his Booke and there you'le see
His whole Designe is Publique Good,
His Soule and Minde an Harmonie.

47
Æt: Suæ
F. H. Van Houe sculp
Johannis Playford Effigies

Appendix VI

Facsimiles of Title Pages from all Known Issues of Playford's *Introduction*

A BIBLIOGRAPHICAL APPENDIX; FACSIMILES OF TITLE PAGES FROM ALL KNOWN ISSUES OF PLAYFORD'S INTRODUCTION

A definitive bibliographical history of Playford's *Introduction to the Skill of Musick* would be beyond the scope and purpose of the present volume. However, it has seemed to the writer essential to provide for the interested reader the means for tracing the development of the series from the first edition of 1654 right through to the last issue of 1730. Through the courtesy of William H. Bond, Houghton Librarian at Harvard, and of his gracious staff, it has been possible to compile the following Appendix, which consists of facsimile title pages from the twenty-three separate issues (not counting the missing ninth edition, which may never have been printed). I am particularly grateful to Miss Judith Andra for generous and excellent assistance. For similar courtesies my thanks also go to the Assistant Music Librarian of the Eda Kuhn Loeb Music Library, Miss Mary Lou Little, and her helpful staff.

A
Breefe
INTRODUCTION
to the Skill
of
MUSICK
for
Song & Violl
by
J P
London Printed
1654
Sould by
Jo: Playford
at his shop
in the Inner
Temple

AN

INTRODUCTION

To the Skill of

MUSICK.

In two Books.

First, a brief & plain *Introduction* to *Musick*, both for *singing*, and for *playing* on the *Viol*. By *J. P.*

Second, The Art of *Setting* or *Composing* of *Musick* in *Parts*, by a most familiar and easie Rule of *Counterpoint*. Formerly published by Dr THO. CAMPION: but now re-printed with large Annotations, By Mr. CHRISTOPH. SYMPSON, and other Additions.

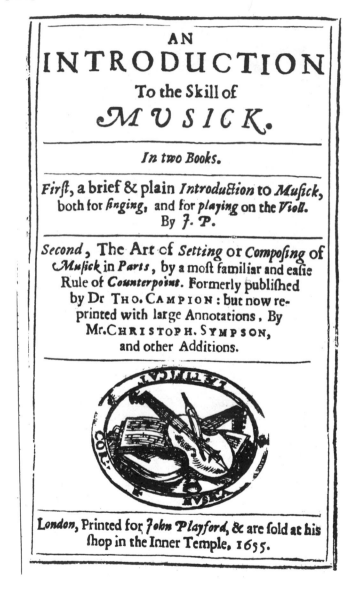

London, Printed for *John Playford*, & are sold at his shop in the Inner Temple, 1655.

A BREIF

INTRODUCTION

To the Skill of

MUSICK:

FOR

SONG and *VIOL*.

In two Books.

First Book contains the *Grounds* and *Rules* of *Musick* for *Song*.

Second Book, *Directions* for the Playing on the *Viol de Gambo*, and also on the *Treble-Violin*.

COR
MVSICA

By *J. Playford*, Philo-Musico.

London, Printed by *W. Godbid*, for *John Playford*, at his Shop in the *Inner-Temple*, neer the Church dore. *M. DC. LVIII.*

A BRIEF

INTRODUCTION

To the Skill of

MUSICK.

In two Books.

The firſt contains the *Grounds* and *Rules* of *MUSICK*.

The ſecond, *Inſtructions* for the *Viol*, and alſo for the *Treble-Violin*.

THE THIRD EDITION Enlarged.

To which is added a Third Book, entituled, The Art of Deſcant, *or* Compoſing MUSICK in Parts, *By Dr.* Tho. Campion. *With Annotations thereon by Mr.* Chr. Simpſon.

CORDI
MUSICA

London, Printed by *W. Godbid* for *John Playford*, at his Shop in the *Inner Temple*, 1660.

A BRIEF

INTRODUCTION

To the Skill of

MUSICK.

In two Books.

The First contains the *Grounds* and *Rules* of *MUSICK.*
The Second, *Instructions* for the *Viol* and also for the *Treble-Violin.*

By *John Playford,* Philo-Musicæ.

To which is added a Third Book, entituled, The Art of Setting, *or* Composing MUSICK in Parts, *By Dr.* Tho. Campion. *With Annotations thereon by Mr.* Chr. Simpson.

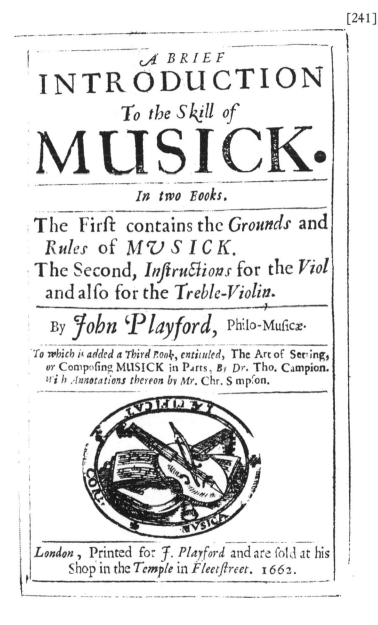

London, Printed for *J. Playford* and are sold at his Shop in the *Temple* in *Fleetstreet.* 1662.

A BRIEF

INTRODUCTION
To the Skill of
MUSICK.

In two Books.

The First containes the General *Grounds* and *Rules* of *MUSICK*.
The Second, *Instructions* for the *Viol* and also for the *Treble-Violin*.

To which is added The Art of Descant, *or* Composing MUSICK in Parts, *By Dr.* Thomas Campion. *With Annotations thereon by Mr.* Chr. Simpson.

The Fourth EDITION much Enlarged.

London, Printed by *William Godbid* for *John Playford,* and are to be sold by *Zach. Watkins,* at their Shop in the *Temple* near the Church-Dore. 1664.

A BRIEF

INTRODUCTION
To the Skill of
MUSICK.

In two Books.

The Firſt containes the General *Grounds* and *Rules* of *MUSICK*.
The Second, *Inſtructions* for the *Viol* and alſo for the *Treble-Violin*.

To which is added The Art of Deſcant, *or* Compoſing MUSICK in Parts, *By Dr.* Thomas Campion. *With Annotations thereon by Mr.* Chr. Simpſon.

London, Printed by *William Godbid* for *John Playford*, and are to be ſold by *Zach. Watkins*, at their Shop in the *Temple* near the Church-Dore. 1664.

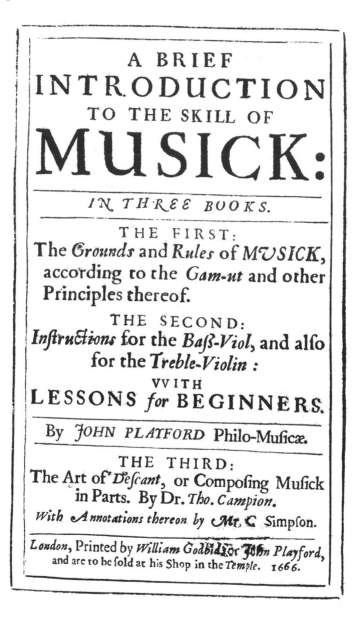

A BRIEF INTRODUCTION TO THE SKILL OF MUSICK:

IN THREE BOOKS.

THE FIRST:
The *Grounds* and *Rules* of *MUSICK*, according to the *Gam-ut* and other Principles thereof.

THE SECOND:
Instructions for the *Bass-Viol*, and also for the *Treble-Violin*:
WITH
LESSONS *for* BEGINNERS.

By *JOHN PLAYFORD* Philo-Musicæ.

THE THIRD:
The Art of *Descant*, or Composing Musick in Parts. By Dr. *Tho. Campion.*
With Annotations thereon by Mr. C Simpson.

London, Printed by *William Godbid* for *John Playford*, and are to be sold at his Shop in the *Temple*. 1666.

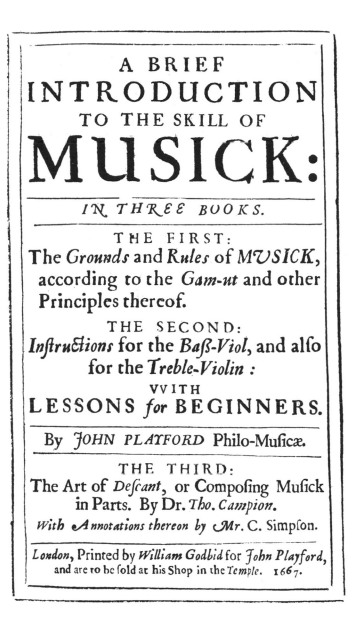

A BRIEF INTRODUCTION TO THE SKILL OF MUSICK:

IN THREE BOOKS.

THE FIRST:
The *Grounds* and *Rules* of *MUSICK*, according to the *Gam-ut* and other Principles thereof.

THE SECOND:
Instructions for the *Bass-Viol*, and also for the *Treble-Violin*:
VVITH
LESSONS *for* BEGINNERS.

By *JOHN PLAYFORD* Philo-Musicæ.

THE THIRD:
The Art of *Descant*, or Composing Musick in Parts. By Dr. *Tho. Campion.*
With Annotations thereon by Mr. C. Simpson.

London, Printed by *William Godbid* for *John Playford*, and are to be sold at his Shop in the *Temple*. 1667.

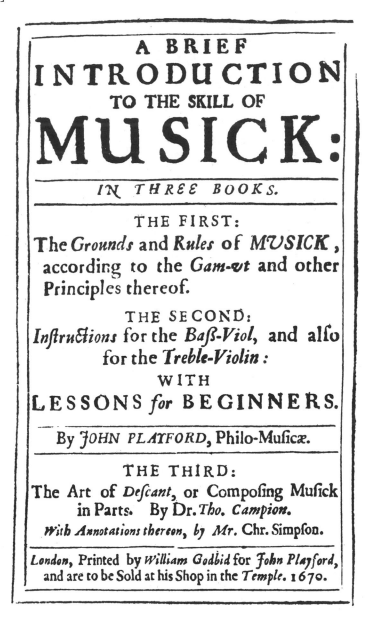

A BRIEF INTRODUCTION TO THE SKILL OF MUSICK:

IN THREE BOOKS.

THE FIRST:
The *Grounds* and *Rules* of *MUSICK*, according to the *Gam-ut* and other Principles thereof.

THE SECOND:
Instructions for the *Bass-Viol*, and also for the *Treble-Violin*:
WITH
LESSONS *for* BEGINNERS.

By *JOHN PLAYFORD*, Philo-Musicæ.

THE THIRD:
The Art of *Descant*, or Composing Musick in Parts. By Dr. *Tho. Campion.*
With Annotations thereon, by Mr. Chr. Simpson.

London, Printed by *William Godbid* for *John Playford*, and are to be Sold at his Shop in the *Temple*. 1670.

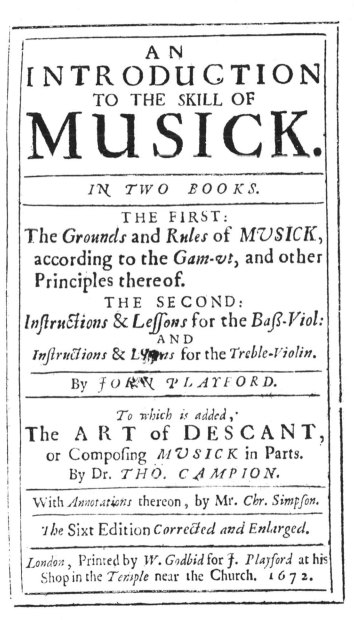

AN INTRODUCTION TO THE SKILL OF MUSICK.

IN TWO BOOKS.

THE FIRST:
The *Grounds* and *Rules* of *MUSICK*, according to the *Gam-ut*, and other Principles thereof.

THE SECOND:
Instructions & *Lessons* for the *Bass-Viol*:
AND
Instructions & *Lessons* for the *Treble-Violin*.

By *JOHN PLAYFORD.*

To which is added,
The ART of DESCANT, or Composing *MUSICK* in Parts.
By Dr. *THO. CAMPION.*

With *Annotations* thereon, by Mr. *Chr. Simpson.*

The Sixt Edition *Corrected and Enlarged.*

London, Printed by *W. Godbid* for *J. Playford* at his Shop in the *Temple* near the Church. 1672.

AN

INTRODUCTION
TO THE SKILL OF

MUSICK.

IN TWO BOOKS.

THE FIRST:
The *Grounds* and *Rules* of *MUSICK*, according to the *Gam-ut*, and other Principles thereof.

THE SECOND:
Instructions & *Lessons* for the *Bass-Viol:*

ctions

AND
Instru~~ments~~s & *Lessons* for the *Treble-Violin.*

By *JOHN PLAYFORD.*

To which is added,
The ART of DESCANT, or Composing *MUSICK* in Parts.
By Dr. *THO. CAMPION.*

With *Annotations* thereon, by Mr. *Chr. Simpson.*

The Seventh Edition, *Corrected and Enlarged.*

London, Printed by *W. Godbid*, for *J. Playford* at his Shop in the *Temple* near the Church. 1674.

AN

INTRODUCTION

TO THE

Skill of Musick.

IN TWO BOOKS.

THE FIRST CONTAINS

The *Grounds* and *Rules* of *MUSICK*, according to the *Gam-ut*, and other *Principles* thereof.

THE SECOND,

INSTRUCTIONS and *LESSONS* both for the BASSE-VIOL and TREBLE-VIOLIN.

By JOHN PLAYFORD.

To which is added,

The ART of *DESCANT*, or Composing of MUSICK in Parts, by Dr. *Tho. Campion*; with *Annotations* thereon by Mr. *Chr. Simpson*.

ALSO

The Order of Singing *Divine Service* in Cathedrals.

The Eighth Edition *carefully Corrected.*

London, Printed by *A. G.* and *J. P.* for *John Playford*, at his Shop in the *Temple* near the Church. 1679.

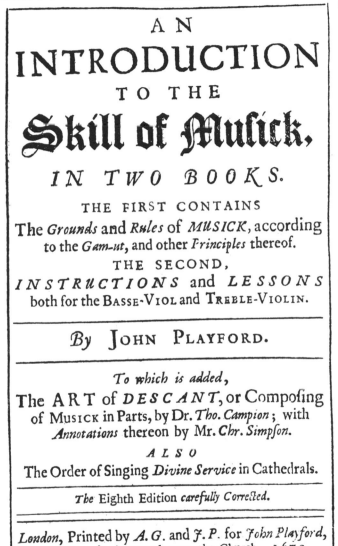

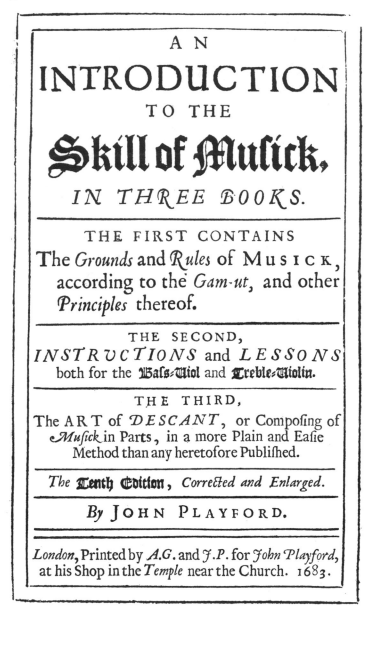

AN

INTRODUCTION

TO THE

Skill of Musick.

IN THREE BOOKS.

THE FIRST CONTAINS

The *Grounds* and *Rules* of MUSICK, according to the *Gam-ut*, and other *Principles* thereof.

THE SECOND,

INSTRUCTIONS and *LESSONS* both for the Bass-Viol and Treble-Violin.

THE THIRD,

The ART of *DESCANT*, or Composing of *Musick* in Parts, in a more Plain and Easie Method than any heretofore Published.

The Tenth Edition, *Corrected and Enlarged.*

By JOHN PLAYFORD.

London, Printed by *A.G.* and *J.P.* for *John Playford*, at his Shop in the *Temple* near the Church. 1683.

AN INTRODUCTION TO THE Skill of Musick,

IN THREE BOOKS.

THE FIRST CONTAINS

The *Grounds* and *Rules* of *MUSICK*, according to the *Gam-ut*, and other *Principles* thereof.

THE SECOND,

INSTRUCTIONS and *LESSONS* both for the Bass-Viol and Treble-Violin.

THE THIRD,

The ART of *DESCANT*, or Composing of *Musick* in Parts, in a more Plain and Easie Method than any heretofore Published.

By JOHN PLAYFORD.

The Eleventh Edition, *Corrected and Enlarged.*

London, Printed by *Charles Peregrine*, for *Henry Playford*, at his Shop near the *Temple* Church, 1687.

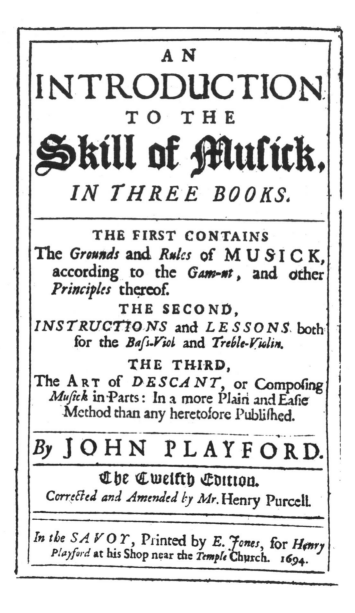

AN

INTRODUCTION TO THE Skill of Musick,

IN THREE BOOKS.

THE FIRST CONTAINS
The *Grounds* and *Rules* of MUSICK, according to the *Gam-ut*, and other *Principles* thereof.

THE SECOND,
INSTRUCTIONS and *LESSONS* both for the *Bass-Viol* and *Treble-Violin*.

THE THIRD,
The ART of *DESCANT*, or Composing *Musick* in Parts: In a more Plain and Easie Method than any heretofore Published.

By JOHN PLAYFORD.

The Twelfth Edition.
Corrected and Amended by Mr. Henry Purcell.

In the SAVOY, Printed by *E. Jones*, for *Henry Playford* at his Shop near the *Temple* Church. 1694.

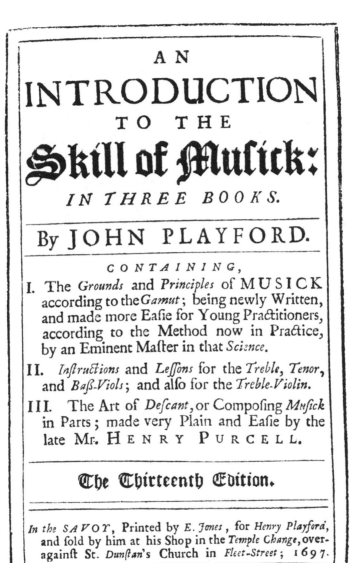

AN

INTRODUCTION TO THE Skill of Musick:

IN THREE BOOKS.

By JOHN PLAYFORD.

CONTAINING,

I. The *Grounds* and *Principles* of MUSICK according to the *Gamut*; being newly Written, and made more Easie for Young Practitioners, according to the Method now in Practice, by an Eminent Master in that *Science*.

II. *Instructions* and *Lessons* for the *Treble*, *Tenor*, and *Bass-Viols*; and also for the *Treble-Violin*.

III. The Art of *Descant*, or Composing *Musick* in Parts; made very Plain and Easie by the late Mr. HENRY PURCELL.

The Thirteenth Edition.

In the SAVOY, Printed by *E. Jones*, for *Henry Playford*, and sold by him at his Shop in the *Temple Change*, over-against St. *Dunstan's* Church in *Fleet-Street*; 1697.

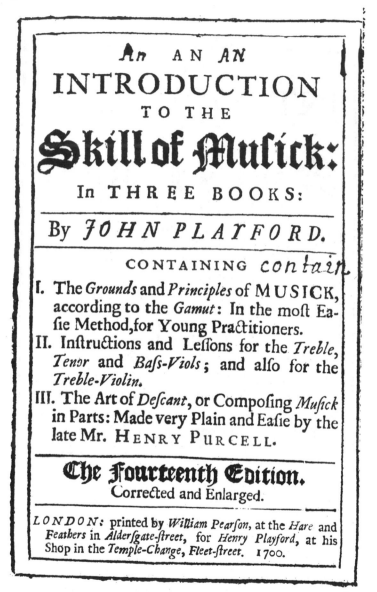

An AN AN

INTRODUCTION
TO THE
Skill of Musick:

In THREE BOOKS:

By *JOHN PLAYFORD.*

CONTAINING contain

I. The *Grounds* and *Principles* of MUSICK, according to the *Gamut*: In the most Easie Method, for Young Practitioners.

II. Instructions and Lessons for the *Treble*, *Tenor* and *Bass-Viols*; and also for the *Treble-Violin*.

III. The Art of *Descant*, or Composing *Musick* in Parts: Made very Plain and Easie by the late Mr. HENRY PURCELL.

The Fourteenth Edition.
Corrected and Enlarged.

LONDON: printed by *William Pearson*, at the *Hare* and *Feathers* in *Aldersgate-street*, for *Henry Playford*, at his Shop in the *Temple-Change*, *Fleet-street*. 1700.

AN

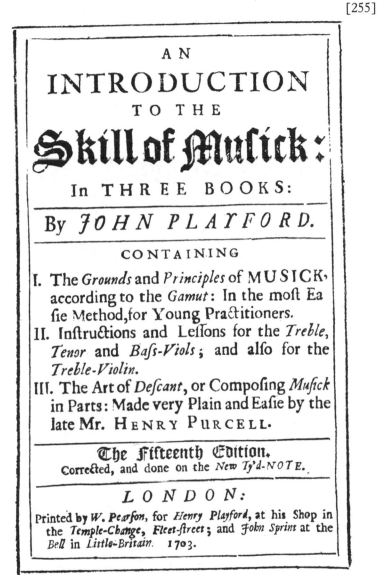

INTRODUCTION
TO THE
Skill of Musick:

In THREE BOOKS:

By *JOHN PLAYFORD.*

CONTAINING

I. The *Grounds* and *Principles* of MUSICK, according to the *Gamut*: In the most Easie Method, for Young Practitioners.

II. Instructions and Lessons for the *Treble*, *Tenor* and *Bass-Viols*; and also for the *Treble-Violin*.

III. The Art of *Descant*, or Composing *Musick* in Parts: Made very Plain and Easie by the late Mr. HENRY PURCELL.

The Fifteenth Edition.
Corrected, and done on the *New Ty'd-NOTE*.

LONDON:

Printed by *W. Pearson*, for *Henry Playford*, at his Shop in the *Temple-Change*, *Fleet-street*; and *John Sprint* at the *Bell* in *Little-Britain*. 1703.

AN

INTRODUCTION TO THE Skill of Musick:

In THREE BOOKS:

By *JOHN PLAYFORD.*

CONTAINING

I. The *Grounds* and *Principles* of MUSICK, according to the *Gamut*: In the moſt Eaſie Method, for Young Practitioners.

II. Inſtructions and Leſſons for the *Treble*, *Tenor*, and *Baſs-Viols*; and alſo for the *Treble Violin*.

III. The Art of *Deſcant*, or Compoſing *Muſick* in Parts: Made very Plain and Eaſie by the late Mr. HENRY PURCELL.

The Sixteenth Edition.
Corrected, and done on the *New Ty'd-NOTE*.

LONDON: Printed by *William Pearſon*, for *John Sprint* at the *Bell* in *Little-Britain*. 1713.

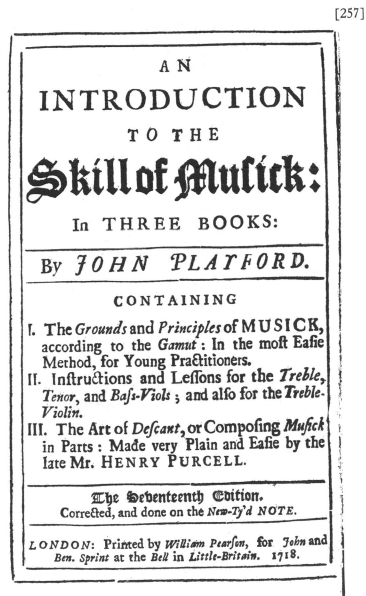

AN

INTRODUCTION

TO THE

Skill of Musick:

In THREE BOOKS:

By *JOHN PLAYFORD.*

CONTAINING

I. The *Grounds* and *Principles* of MUSICK, according to the *Gamut*: In the most Easie Method, for Young Practitioners.

II. Instructions and Lessons for the *Treble*, *Tenor*, and *Bass-Viols*; and also for the *Treble-Violin*.

III. The Art of *Descant*, or Composing *Musick* in Parts: Made very Plain and Easie by the late Mr. HENRY PURCELL.

The Seventeenth Edition.
Corrected, and done on the *New-Ty'd NOTE*.

LONDON: Printed by *William Pearson*, for *John* and *Ben. Sprint* at the *Bell* in *Little-Britain*. 1718.

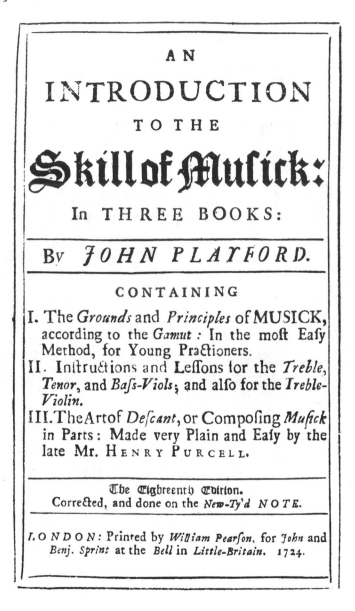

AN

INTRODUCTION

TO THE

Skill of Musick:

In THREE BOOKS:

By *JOHN PLAYFORD.*

CONTAINING

I. The *Grounds* and *Principles* of MUSICK, according to the *Gamut*: In the most Easy Method, for Young Practioners.

II. Instructions and Lessons for the *Treble, Tenor*, and *Bass-Viols*; and also for the *Treble-Violin.*

III. The Art of *Descant*, or Composing *Musick* in Parts: Made very Plain and Easy by the late Mr. HENRY PURCELL.

The Eighteenth Edition.
Corrected, and done on the *New-Ty'd* NOTE.

LONDON: Printed by *William Pearson*, for *John* and *Benj. Sprint* at the *Bell* in *Little-Britain*. 1724.

AN INTRODUCTION TO THE Skill of Musick:

In THREE BOOKS:

By *JOHN PLAYFORD*.

CONTAINING

I. The *Grounds* and *Principles* of MUSICK, according to the *Gamut*: In the most Easy Method, for Young Practitioners.

II. Instructions and Lessons for the *Treble Tenor*, and *Bass-Viols*; and also for the *Treble-Violin*.

III. The Art of *Descant*, or Composing *Musick* in Parts: Made very Plain and Easy by the late Mr. HENRY PURCELL.

The Nineteenth Edition.
Corrected, and done on the *New-Ty'd NOTE*.

LONDON: Printed by *William Pearson*, for *Benjamin Sprint* at the *Bell* in *Little-Britain*. MDCCXXX.

Glossary of Musical Terms

A SHORT AND CONCISE GLOSSARY OF MUSICAL TERMS USED IN THE FOREGOING TREATISE IN SPECIAL OR UNUSUAL SENSES

AFFECT (or Affection, *cf.* Doctrine of the Affections; *Affektenlehre*): Musical counterparts of passion or active emotions.

AYRE ("Air"): A term with several meanings. In its most common usage (as on pp. 31 and 41) the term denotes a melodic song for one or more voices with instrumental accompaniment, frequently such a song in a cantata or opera. A second seventeenth-century meaning, denoting "an instrumental tune," was not used by Playford in the *Introduction.* A third use of the term is that given on page 106, its meaning being "key of the tune" or "melodic tonality." Thomas Morley (1557–1603) used the term in this sense in his treatise, *A Plain and Easy Introduction to Practical Music,* as follows:

> But when you would express a lamentable passion then you must use motions proceeding by half notes, flat thirds, and flat sixths, which of their nature are sweet, specially being taken in the true tune and natural air with discretion and judgement.*

In the passage on page 115, Purcell seems to have equated the term "Air" with tunefulness.

B-DURALIS (♮): The hard or square-shaped B (*i.e.,* B-natural), third note in the "hard" hexachord beginning on G. See Gamut.

B-MOLLARIS (♭): The soft, or round-shaped "B" (*i.e.,* B-flat), fourth note in the "soft" hexachord beginning on F. See Gamut.

BACKFALL: Short grace-note or short appoggiatura played one degree above the written note.

BREVE: From the Latin "brevis" meaning short, originally the smaller division of the "long" (longa). In seventeenth-century music the "breve" occurs mainly at the ends of compositions and in

*Modern edition (London, Dent, 1952), p. 290.

certain "tripla" passages with a time signature equivalent to modern $\frac{3}{1}$.

CLOSE: Cadence as a terminating harmonic/melodic device in phrase, period, section, or movement. A "half close" corresponds more or less to the modern imperfect cadence, the "full close" to the perfect cadence.

COMPASS: Range, referring mainly to upper and lower limits, and not to tessitura.

CONCEIT: Term relating to the ideas contained in the text of a song relating to the author's conception, notion, or device.

CONSORT: Chamber ensemble: The simple term "consort" frequently was used in seventeenth-century England to refer to "broken (*i.e.,* "mixed") consort," even to ensembles in which voices took part, and sometimes to the musicians themselves.

CORANT: English term for the running dance (or *danse courante*) of France or for the simpler Italian *coranto* or *corrente.* Morley, who uses the French spelling in his *A Plain and Easy Introduction to Practical Music* (p. 297), speaks of the *courante* as a dance of trevising (*i.e.,* traversing) and running, in the measure of the English country dance.

COUNTERPOINT: Although currently in general use to denote a tonal compositional procedure related to, but more strictly formal than polyphonic imitation, the term "counterpoint" appears to have a very special sense in this edition of Playford's treatise. All the examples given would now be termed "note-against-note" counterpoint. The example on page 101 suggests that the term also connotes contrary-motion, while that on page 115 indicates that "counterpoint" may be distinguishable from its polyphonic equivalent (*stile famigliare*) by its tunefulness or, as Purcell put it, "good Air." See also Ayre and Fuge or Pointing.

CROTCHET: A quarter-note.

DESCANT: In Playford's treatise, particularly as used by the anonymous author of the "Brief Discourse of the Italian manner of Singing," the term seems to denote the art of uniting melodies according to the rules of interval preparation and resolution. In double descant (see p. 113), two parts are written so that either may be sung above or below the other without infraction of these rules. (For five other meanings of the term, see J. A. Westrup and

F. L. Harrison, *The New College Encyclopedia of Music* (New York, Norton, 1960), p. 184.)

DIAPASON (literally "of all") : Octave.

DIVISION: Melodic and rhythmic elaboration or ornamentation of a tune. "Division" may be accomplished, either instrumentally or vocally, by dividing large intervals into smaller ones, by dividing long notes into shorter rhythmic units or patterns, or by a combination of these two procedures. More particularly, the term was used in seventeenth-century England to refer to variations on a ground.

EIGHTS: Octaves.

FUGE: As used in this treatise, the term refers to imitative counterpoint, as distinct from the modern term "fugue." (See also Imitation and Reports for contrasting terms.) In seventeenth-century England, the term was used mainly to denote a general technique, not a form or structure. Modern usage distinguishes between imitative counterpoint, which was tonally conceived, and imitative polyphony, which was primarily modal. For the latter, see also Imitation and Reports.

GAMUT: The scalar system in which the twenty diatonic tones from G (*i.e.,* Gamma ut in ancient terminology) to e, plus two varieties of B, were divided into seven hexachords, or "deductions" as follows:

G A B c d e
c d e f g a
f g a b♭[1] c d
c d e f g a
f g a b♭[1] c d
g a b♮[2] c d e

1. B-mollaris (*q.v.*)
2. B-duralis (*q.v.*)

Natural hexachords are those without "B"; soft hexachords are those with B-flat; hard hexachords are those with B-natural.

GRACES: Melodic ornaments.

HARMONY: In Playford's *Introduction* the term is used both to denote the individual chord (p. 32) and the harmonic progression (p. 85).

IMITATION: Polyphonic "point imitation." See also Reports.

KEY WITH FLAT THIRD: Minor key.

KEY WITH SHARP THIRD: Major key.

LARGE: Very long note value, equivalent to as many as eighty-one quarter notes.

LESSON: A musical piece. By Purcell's time the term was reserved for short compositions for harpsichord or other solo instrument.

LONG: From the Latin "longa;" a note value already obsolete in the seventeenth century, its normal value was equivalent to that of twenty-seven quarter notes.

LYRA-WAY (or "Harp-way"): Written in tablature (*i.e.,* schematic diagrams denoting positions on the fingerboard and intended for a viol tuned in a special way).

MASTER-NOTE: As used on page nine, synonymous with "leading tone"; as used on page twenty-one, synonymous with "whole note," then a new term for the semibreve (*q.v.*).

MEAN: The part (vocal or instrumental) between soprano (or cantus, or treble) and tenor; earlier, the middle part in a three-voice keyboard piece.

MINIM: Half note.

MOOD: Mensural designation showing relationship between long and breve, as "time" shows that between breve and semibreve and "prolation" that between semibreve, minim, and smaller values. In every case a "perfect" relationship indicated that the larger value contained three of the next smaller, while an "imperfect" relationship indicated that it contained two. Playford's subdivisions on page twenty-one are all "imperfect." See also Proportion.

POINTING: Technique for the formulation of imitative counterpoint. (See also Counterpoint, Imitation, and Reports). Not to be confused with the nineteenth-century use of the term, having to do with the fitting of notes to syllables in Anglican chant.

PROPORTION: Term denoting rhythmic relationships between various note values. The proportion was "perfect" if the ratio was three to one, "imperfect" if two to one. See also Mood.

QUAVER: Eighth note.

Glossary

REPORTS: Simple polyphonic imitation, as distinguished by Purcell from contrapuntal (*i.e.,* tonal) imitation.

SEMIBREVE: Whole note.

SEMI-QUAVER: Sixteenth note.

SHAKE: Trill.

TABLATURE: Schematic diagram or symbol system denoting positions on fingerboard or keyboard.

THEORBO: Small bass lute used for figured bass realization.

TRIPLA-TIME: $\frac{3}{2}$ or $\frac{3}{4}$ or even $\frac{3}{1}$.

Index

Index

N